THE QUEST

FOR THE OTHER

ETHNIC TOURISM

IN SAN CRISTÓBAL,

MEXICO

ETHNIC

TOURISM

IN SAN

CRISTÓBAL,

MEXICO

PIERRE L. VAN DEN BERGHE

UNIVERSITY OF

WASHINGTON PRESS

SEATTLE & LONDON

THE QUEST FOR THE OTHER

Library of Congress
Cataloging-in-Publication Data
Van den Berghe, Pierre L.
    The quest for the other : ethnic
tourism in San Cristóbal, Mexico /
Pierre L. Van den Berghe.
    p.   cm.
    Includes bibliographical references
and index.
    ISBN 0-295-97317-X
    1. Tourist trade—Mexico—San
Cristóbal de las Casas.   2. Indians
of Mexico—Mexico—San Cristóbal
de las Casas—Social life and
customs.   I. Title.
G155.M6v36   1994
338.4'7917275—dc20   93-40687
                                       CIP

To Gonzalo Aguirre Beltrán,

whose *Regiones de Refugio* (1967)

remains, after a quarter century,

the theoretical master key to

understanding Mexican ethnic

relations and the Chiapas highlands.

CONTENTS

ACKNOWLEDGMENTS

Like Dean MacCannell in his famous book, *The Tourist* (1976; second edition, 1989), I take great pleasure in not having to thank any funding agency for underwriting this study. The only institutional support it received was my reduced salary during a sabbatical leave from the University of Washington. This study is thus my first substantial piece of fieldwork done and written without any strings attached, and without any concern for career consequences. In short, this is the work of a free man. I am free to publish and be damned.

I take, however, great pleasure in acknowledging my human and intellectual debts, for they were freely incurred and gladly received. In good anthropological fashion, I want to thank the entire population of San Cristóbal de las Casas for their kindness, courtesy, and hospitality. More than any other fieldwork setting I encountered in half a dozen countries, San Cristóbal has been a home away from home. I have known the town for over thirty years, and developed a number of valued friendships and associations during visits in 1959, 1966, 1972, 1977, 1987, and 1990. More than anyone, the late Prudencio Moscoso Pastrana and his wife Gloria have been not only hospitable friends but real collaborators. Prudencio Moscoso was perhaps the most knowledgeable historian of the region, and his mind (backed by his impressive library) was an inexhaustible source of data. Leopoldo Velasco, his wife Carmen, and their daughter Socorro have likewise been valued friends and gracious hosts, as have Bob and Mimi Laughlin. Bob's and Mimi's expertise on the region is also boundless, and their gorgeously restored old house was a frequent setting for meeting other fascinating people. At the risk of being selective, I would also like to thank Magdalena Mandujano Santiago and Lucía Méndez Toporek, employees of the Oficina de Turismo, who gave me full access to their data and cheerfully put up with my frequent and inquisitive presence in their office; Joaquín Hernanz Humbias, old friend and owner of the oldest tourist-oriented store in San Cristóbal, and his son, José Antonio, the hotelier; Sergio Castro, a former teacher in Indian villages who collects regional textiles and now acts as a tour guide; the historian Jan de Vos, creator of the superb INAH museum; the anthropologist Armando Aguirre Torres of the Instituto Nacional Indígenista; the physician Pablo González Casanova (son of the famous sociologist), with whom I talked a lot about Africa; the journalist Hans Matthai, who was also doing work on tourism, in Na Bolom; the anthropologist Jan Rus, my companion in Chamula; and Hilda Urbina Zepeda, a hotel manager who introduced me to the world of hotelkeeping.

The 175 tourists of nineteen different nationalities who responded to my request for an interview showed not only an extraordinary amount of cooperation, but, in many cases, good cheer and companionship which extended into a pleasant relationship lasting several hours or even an entire day. Since most of them traveled with companions, and since I talked to a number of tourists besides those I formally interviewed, perhaps some 400 tourists contributed data to this study. Many turned out to be very sophisticated, charming, and interesting human beings.

I would like to put in a "plug" for the Hotel Posada de San Cristóbal, my home near the Zócalo. Its modest two stars give but a faint idea of its charm. It is located in the poetically named Casa de las Sirenas, a massive colonial building with meter-thick adobe walls, nearly a half millennium old. Its placid patio was an ideal place to write my field notes, yet it was only fifty meters from the bustle of the Zócalo. It was also in the same building that I spent my first night in San Cristóbal as an eager twenty-six-year-old graduate student about to undertake his first piece of anthropological fieldwork. I have come full circle.

After my return to Seattle, my graduate student, Joe Whitmeyer, transferred my coded interviews to a computer program, and is thus largely responsible for ordering the quantitative data in Chapter 4. One of these days I may yet overcome my phobia of computers, but people of Joe's competence help me postpone the day of reckoning, and I am truly grateful. My debt to Peter Kelley, Ann Prentice, Roberta Rogers, and Catherine Frakes, who transformed my scribblings into a usable typescript, is much greater than average.

Lastly, the final text is an improved version that received the benefit of highly informed, insightful, and constructive comments by a number of readers. My warmest thanks to Jafar Jafari, Bob Laughlin, Dean Mac-Cannell, Kevin Neuhouser, Valene L. Smith, and Joe Whitmeyer.

Pierre van den Berghe
Seattle, May 1993

THE QUEST

FOR THE OTHER

ETHNIC TOURISM

IN SAN CRISTÓBAL,

MEXICO

WHY STUDY ETHNIC TOURISM?

1   INTRODUCTION

Judging by the smirk which the mere mention of tourism brings to the face of my colleagues, most social scientists do not take tourism seriously. Anthropologists are perhaps a little less ready to dismiss the topic as frivolous than are sociologists, and some economists recognize it as the massive worldwide industry that it is. Nonetheless, most of my colleagues strongly imply that a professed interest in tourism constitutes little more than a clever ploy to pass off one's vacations as work. I would not deny that the study of tourism is great fun, but must a subject be boring to be worthy of study? By now, enough fascinating work on tourism and its products (such as tourist arts) has been produced to document that tourism is not only a phenomenon of gigantic import in the modern world but also one presenting intellectually challenging problems.[1] Therefore, I shall not apologize; rather I shall show why I came to study the particular kind of tourism that I am interested in—ethnic tourism, in this particular location—San Cristóbal de las Casas, on the highlands of the state of Chiapas, in southeastern Mexico.

WHO IS A TOURIST?

First, what is tourism and who is a tourist? Almost any treatise, anthology, or review article on tourism starts with a definitional exercise and a taxonomy of types of tourism (Cohen 1972, 1974; de Kadt 1979; Graburn 1983; MacCannell 1976; Smith 1989; Wahab 1975). I seek to avoid pedantry, but the boundaries of tourism are not as self-evident as they might first appear, and obviously any study must be empirically bounded. Let us start with a simple definition: tourism is traveling for pleasure. But how far must one travel to become a tourist? Around the corner? To the next town? To a foreign country? There is obviously such a thing as "domestic tourism," and I certainly included Mexicans in my definition of tourism in San Cristóbal. In fact, there is no clear boundary between national and international tourism. Most countries are sufficiently diverse that one can easily duplicate an exotic, foreign experience close to home. To the citizen of Albuquerque, the Navajo Reservation can be as exotic as San Juan Chamula. At the limit, a subway trip to an ethnic restaurant or to a foreign movie can be seen as a minitourist experience. Somewhat arbitrarily, however, and for purposes of convenience, let us define the tourist as having to come from a different community, either in space or in culture.

That leaves us with the problem of defining pleasure. Many of us find

1. See Cohen 1974, 1979a, 1979b; de Kadt 1979; Graburn 1976, 1983, 1989; Jafari 1979, 1987; MacCannell 1973, 1976; Nash 1981; Smith 1989; Turner and Ash 1976; and the pages of the *Annals of Tourism Research*, for a short beginner's bibliography. Useful review articles on tourism in the various social sciences are found in volume 18, number 1, 1991, of the *Annals*, especially Graburn and Jafari (1991), Dann and Cohen (1991), and Nash and Smith (1991). See also the older articles by Cohen (1972, 1979a, 1984), Graburn (1983), and Nash (1981).

pleasure in work, and even find it difficult to differentiate work and play. However, and again somewhat arbitrarily, let us define tourism as a leisure-time activity engaged in by choice and for its own sake. When I am studying tourism as an anthropologist, I may look like a tourist— that is, I may blend in quite well as a participant observer—but I am not really a tourist, because I have an ulterior motive beyond simply being there for its own sake.

Even so, the definitional problem is not entirely solved, because leisure and work often overlap. Is the American physician at a medical conference in Bermuda a tourist or a conventioneer? I would probably a bit of both, and it would depend on her behavior while there. Obviously, many people combine business and pleasure on trips, and can be both tourists and nontourists on the same trip. I encountered a few in my sample, like the young long-haired musicians and artists who finance their wanderlust by playing the guitar in tourist restaurants or selling their costume jewelry in the tourist market. Yet the borderline in nearly all cases is fairly clear-cut. The young American motorcyclist, for instance, who financed his long Mexican trip by distributing leaflets for flying ambulance services in resorts full of elderly Americans was clearly a tourist. He wanted to see Mexico; he was not distributing leaflets as a profession. On the other hand, the Guatemalan merchant who comes to San Cristóbal to sell textiles to other travelers is clearly not a tourist, though he lives from tourism. Nonetheless, a few marginal cases make the problem interesting. How about the young Dutchman traveling on behalf of his brother who owns a craft shop in Amsterdam, and who buys thousands of dollars worth of crafts for shipment to Holland? His prime motivation was to see Mexico and learn Spanish, but he was certainly in business as well, albeit somewhat vicariously.

What is clear, however, is that it is not objective behavior by itself that defines tourist status. Certain actions (such as taking pictures, reading tourist guides, not knowing prices) provide clues as to whether a person is a tourist or not, but they do not define the tourist. When I took photographs of Indians in the tourist market in San Cristóbal, I could easily have been mistaken for a tourist, but that behavior did not make me a tourist. It is thus the subjective motive of the person that makes him a tourist or not. Perhaps the broadest model of what transforms a person into a tourist is taking a leap out of ordinary life (Jafari 1987).

The tourism scene can thus be seen as the intersection of the tourist's extraordinary world with the host's ordinary life.

Now, however, we stumble into another problem. Is self-proclamation as a tourist a sufficient condition for being one? In most cases, probably yes. The reciprocal, however, is not true. Denial of tourist status does not exclude one. Most tourists seek authenticity (Cohen 1988; MacCannell 1976; van den Berghe and Keyes 1984), and the presence of tourists destroys authenticity. Therefore, most tourists resent other tourists, and many reject the very label. Indeed, the label "tourist" is less than two centuries old, even though the activity of traveling for pleasure is millennia old.[2] Tourism was only labeled such when the railways and steamships of the nineteenth century made it a mass experience. Before, we had explorers, adventurers, travelers, crusaders, pilgrims. Yet, by our definition, they too were tourists (Smith 1992). That is, their behavior was similarly motivated: they were traveling for their own satisfaction of nonutilitarian goals. The ludic element is a common denominator of tourism (Jafari 1987). Tourism is but one of the many manifestations of the enormous human capacity for being playful (Huizinga 1955).

Travel implies transience, and that gets us into another problem of definition. How transient does a tourist have to be? How long a stay does it take to stop being a tourist? Any cutoff point is arbitrary. My data suggest that a six-month stay is a good discriminant, but a person coming with the intention of staying a long time, and, say, leasing a house for a year instead of staying in a hotel, can stop being a tourist in perhaps three months or less. In San Cristóbal, the line between foreign tourists and resident gringos was rather clear, especially to the latter category, who emphatically rejected the tourist label, and showed irritation when locals (such as street vendors) failed to make the distinction. Yet the very fact that, to many natives, the differentiation was not clear points to a conceptual problem. Do you stop being a tourist when you think so, or when others stop treating you as one?

In practice, I seldom had difficulty in determining who was a tourist,

2. "Tourist" first appears in print as an English noun in 1800, and "tourism" in 1811, but the neologisms did not spread until later in the century, when the phenomenon itself became more massive (Ginier 1969).

using almost exclusively external behavioral or phenotypic clues, and in the vast majority of cases my guess was validated by the self-definition of the person picked. Initially, I occasionally mistook resident gringos for tourists, but they are few enough in number and they behave sufficiently differently that after a couple of weeks any confusion disappeared. The other marginal cases concerned Mexicans, and I discuss some cases in Chapter 2. Even persons rejecting the label of tourist, and calling themselves "travelers," or, in one case, "pilgrim," recognized their pretense as a semantic quibble, and did not object to being included in what I clearly identified as a study of tourism. (See Riley 1988:322 for rejection of the "tourist" label by "long-term, low-budget travelers.") In operational terms, then, a tourist in this study was anyone I thought behaved or looked like one, and accepted that definition when approached as a potential respondent in what I explicitly stated to be a study of tourism. (See Chapter 2 for an explicit list of criteria of inclusion.)

WHAT IS ETHNIC TOURISM?

My interest is not so much in tourism in general, however, as in ethnic tourism. Along with indulging in cute definitional exercises, students of tourism delight in taxonomy. There are approximately as many qualifiers of tourism as there are authors in the field: sun-sand-and-sea tourism, adventure tourism, ecotourism, nature tourism, sex tourism, cultural tourism, backpack tourism, package tours, alternative tourism, counterculture tourism, long-term-low-budget tourism, trekking tourism, and so on. Some of these types are based on the tourist attractant, others on tourist attributes, others on tourist lifestyles, and still others merely on geography (such as "photographic safari," an exercise which the Swahili term confines to Africa). Some forms of tourism are merely adaptations of hobbies also conducted at home (photography, bird watching, hiking, and so forth), or sports for which the home environment is not suitable (skiing, scuba diving, mountain climbing). The variations, in short, are infinite, and no taxonomy can be exhaustive.

Nevertheless, some types of tourism have special characteristics that make them especially interesting to study. My favorite type is what I and others have called ethnic tourism (Cazes 1989; Graburn 1989; Smith 1989; van den Berghe 1980; van den Berghe and Keyes 1984; Weiler and Hall 1992; Wood 1984). Tourism is always, in some sense, a form of ethnic relations, for it puts into contact people who are strangers to one another, and who invariably belong to different cultures or subcultures. Tourists of different nationalities themselves constitute a multiethnic group, yet the commonalities of the tourist situation weld them into a temporary kind of "super-ethny." At least, natives often look at them as a relatively undifferentiated mass in relation to their hosts (Jafari 1984).

What differentiates ethnic tourism from other types is not simply that tourism is a form of ethnic relations, for all tourism is that. Rather, what defines ethnic tourism is the nature of the tourist attractant: ethnic tourism exists where the tourist actively searches for ethnic exoticism. In Weiler and Hall's (1992:84) definition, ethnic tourism is "travel motivated primarily by the search for the first hand, authentic and sometimes intimate contact with people whose ethnic and/or cultural background is different from the tourist's." In MacCannell's terms, tourism is a product of modernity (MacCannell 1976). Modernity produces homogenization, instability, and inauthenticity, and thus generates in the most modernized among us a quest for the opposite of these things. The tourist searches for authentic encounters with the other. The greater the otherness of the other, the more satisfying the tourist experience. At the limit, this makes anthropology the ultimate form of tourism.

MacCannell probably overgeneralizes a frequent, yet far from universal, motivation among tourists. Not all tourists seek *dépaysement*, as the French say (Nash 1984). Many are threatened by it and seek, on the contrary, the security of familiar food served by people fluent in their language in the familiar setting of an "international" hotel with only the most subdued reminders of location. Many tourists feel secure only when they move in the aseptic, air-conditioned bubble of the luxury bus and hotel, and tolerate only sanitized versions of cultural exotica: the native dancers have to come to the Hilton to perform their choreographed bit of "staged authenticity" (MacCannell 1973). The cultural other is only a faint backdrop which barely enables one to distinguish the Bangkok Hilton from the Bangor one. The glow of foreign ethnicity is reduced to a mural in the reception lobby and the pigmentation of the hotel and restaurant personnel, suitably attired in pseudotraditional dress. Many North Americans, for instance, like places such as the interior of Baja California because there they find Mexico without Mexicans. The great success of the Club Méditerranée is that it resolutely excludes the locals from its secluded, manicured, sanitized precincts—except, of course, as servants. Only servility makes the native acceptable to many tourists. The Club Méditerranée is successful because it is modernity incarnate, not because it offers an escape from modernity.

Yet MacCannell is quite correct that many tourists actively seek *dépaysement* and cultural exoticism. What I term "ethnic tourism" is the prototype of this search for the other. The ethnic tourist is the one who actively searches for the ethnically exotic, in as untouched, pristine, authentic a form as he can find it. (See Cohen 1973, 1979b, 1979c, 1987, 1988; Esman 1984; Graburn 1976, 1983, 1989; Laxson 1991; MacCannell 1976, 1984; Smith 1989; Swain 1990.) This tourist wants unspoiled natives, not bilingual waiters and beachboys. The native is not merely a host, a provider of creature comforts, a servant, but becomes, quite literally, the spectacle. The native becomes what I have called the "touree" (van den Berghe 1980). As an object of curiosity, the touree is on show, whether he wants to be or not; he must make a spectacle of himself. But he remains authentic only as long as he does not consciously modify his behavior to make himself more attractive to tourists. Therein lies the great irony of ethnic tourism: it is self-destroying. The presence of tourists spoils the tourees. The tourists must forever push beyond the waves of spoilage created by their intrusion, in search of more and more remote Shangri-las, just beyond the reach of the bulldozer and on the heels of the missionary and the anthropologist. The live fringe of ethnic tourism is the outer reach of the second-class bus. Like the advancing line of a savannah fire, it consumes the commodity it searches: the authentic other.[3]

3. The literature on ethnic tourism, though not always labeled as such, is quickly expanding. Much of it can be found in the pages of the *Annals of Tourism Research*, especially the following: Adams 1984; Altman 1989; Brewer

The prime tourees are the Fourth World peoples (Graburn 1976), the marginal communities who live on the fringes of their respective "national" societies (which can be First, Second, or Third World).[4] Frequently, tourees have been able to preserve their otherness only through geographical isolation in what the Mexican anthropologist Gonzalo Aguirre Beltrán (1979) has called "regions of refuge," often remote mountain areas, jungles, or deserts largely devoid of valuable resources warranting the cost of creating access. Fourth World peoples occupy the last remnants of a planet which the capitalist world system had not yet found worth exploiting. That last refuge from modernity is now being invaded by ethnic tourism.

In a sense, ethnic tourism represents the last wave of exploitative capitalist expansion into the remotest periphery of the world system, to use Wallerstein's (1974) terminology. Fourth World peoples who were first pushed back into regions of refuge—the "native reserves" of the colonized—are now being "rediscovered" as a tourist resource. Their prior isolation from the mainstream of their respective dominant societies has transformed them into objects of curiosity and nostalgia for the affluent in search of the exotic (Cohen 1982a; Riley 1988; Vogt 1976). Now, even poverty becomes an exploitable commodity if it is colorful enough. The most inaccessible cultures and peoples are being commoditized (Cohen 1988).

1984; Britton 1979; Bruner 1989; Cohen 1973, 1979a, 1979b, 1979c, 1982a, 1989; Esman 1984; Evans-Pritchard 1989; Kemper 1978, 1981; Keyes and van den Berghe 1984; and Laxson, 1991. See also de Kadt 1979; Graburn 1976; Kottak 1983; Nash 1989; Singh 1989; Smith 1989; Turner and Ash 1976; van den Berghe 1980; Volkman 1982, 1984; Wahrlich 1984.

4. The term Third World is a French coinage (*Tiers Monde*), by analogy to the Third Estate in the prerevolutionary Estates General. Third World refers to the poor, largely agrarian countries which are neither advanced capitalist countries (First World) nor advanced Socialist countries (Second World). The label Fourth World has referred either to the poorest of the poor countries (e.g., Nepal, Burkina Faso, Rwanda, or Haiti), or to enclaved, marginalized, stigmatized groups within First, Second, or Third World countries. It is this second meaning that I shall use here.

As it happens, the highlands of Chiapas served as the archetype of Aguirre Beltrán's region of refuge, and thus are an especially appropriate setting for a study of ethnic tourism. The Chiapas highlands are the largest area inhabited by monolingual Indians left in Mexico, although bilingualism is now advancing fast. The highlands include in a single large pocket close to one-tenth of the 12 million or so Mexicans classified as Indians because they are still native speakers of indigenous languages. Collectively, these 12 million Indians make up some 14 percent of the Mexican population of 85 million. They constitute fifty-six recognized ethnies or micronations living in the interstices of the Spanish-speaking, mestizo society that dominates the Mexican state and economy, and claims to represent the "national" culture.

The local representatives of the mestizo society of Chiapas call themselves ladinos, an old colonial term referring to speakers of Spanish. It is a term Chiapas mestizos share with their Guatemalan counterparts, although increasingly the term "mestizo" is also used locally (figs. 6, 7, 8, and 9). The dominant Chiapas elite probably share more of a regional subculture with Guatemala than with the rest of Mexico. Chiapas Indians, on the other hand, are speakers of several related Mayan languages, especially Tzotzil and Tzeltal in the vicinity of San Cristóbal (figs. 10, 11, 12, and 13). The Indian groups of Chiapas are also closely related to the Maya groups of Guatemala. Indeed, some of these groups straddle the Mexico-Guatemala boundary.

Since the Conquest of the 1520s, the Spaniards who, after several generations of intermixture with Indians, started calling themselves mestizos or ladinos have dominated the region, and indeed the whole of Mexico and Central America. San Cristóbal was founded as Villa Real de Chiapa in 1528 by Diego de Mazariegos, the conquistador who now has a hotel named after him, and a statue near the church of Santo Domingo (fig. 5). The other great historical figure of the early colonial period was San Cristóbal's first bishop, Fray Bartolomé de las Casas, whose name was appended to that of the town, when it became San Cristóbal de las Casas in 1848 (de Vos 1986). While his tenure in the bishop's see did not exceed a few weeks in 1545, his

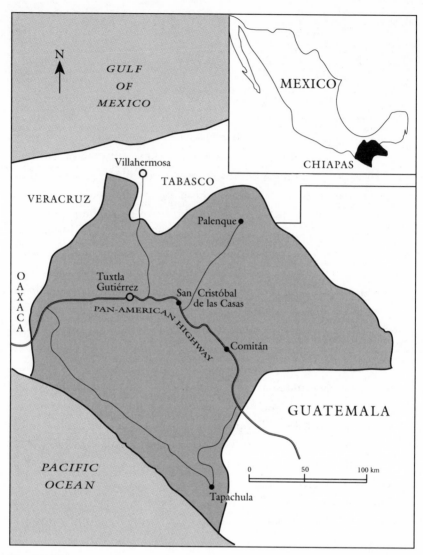

Map 1. Chiapas

fame as "defender of the Indians" lasted. He, too, rates a hotel, and San Cristóbal erected to him two statues, the newer one on the Pan-American Highway and a smaller, older one a few blocks from the Zócalo. San Cristóbal is probably unique among Mexican towns in having three statues to Spaniards, and none to the usual heroes of the independence pantheon (except for inconspicuous busts back of the Town Hall). Not only in its architecture, San Cristóbal remains a colonial city with a conservative elite and a highly hierarchical class and ethnic structure.

The Fourth World peoples who are attractive to ethnic tourists are often at a disadvantage in "selling" themselves directly to the tourists, although they may be quick to exploit new economic niches open to them for the "commoditization" of themselves and their artifacts. Thus they start demanding fees for being photographed, or producing artifacts more or less distantly related to their "traditional" ones for sale to tourists. However, in the typical situation, such as that of the Chiapas highlands, where the tourees live in a region dominated politically, culturally, and economically by representatives of the "national" culture, the tourees are handicapped in selling themselves directly to tourists. This is true for several obvious reasons:

1. They speak languages unrelated to those of the tourists; and these are languages too limited in their diffusion to be learned by many outsiders.

2. Their limited access to formal Western schooling, at least beyond the lower primary grades, slows down their acquisition of the cultural and linguistic skills of the dominant "national" culture. Thus the paradox: they are interesting because they are unacculturated to the dominant group, but their lack of acculturation handicaps them in marketing their exoticism to tourists.

3. The geographical remoteness and isolation that preserve their exoticism also put them beyond the reach of most tourist services, such as hotels and restaurants. In most cases, they live in peasant villages visited by tourists on day trips from larger urban centers dominated by local elites from the "national" culture.

4. Most of the touree contacts with tourists take place when the touree comes to town to sell, either agricultural goods or tourist artifacts. The interaction, however, takes place in a social arena controlled by local

representatives of the "national" culture, where the tourees are in a subordinate position.

By contrast, members of the dominant "national" culture are much less interesting to ethnic tourists, especially in a country like Mexico where mestizos are seen by Europeans and North Americans as basically Westerners, carriers of an American variant of Hispanic culture. However, the dominant group is in a much better position to market and commoditize the touree than the touree is himself.

1. Local elites have access to secondary and tertiary education (including specialized schools geared to training people in the tourist industry), and consequently have much greater opportunities to learn at least a smattering of the principal European languages spoken by the majority of tourists: English, French, and German.

2. They live in the towns where tourists are housed, and thus have ample opportunities to observe tourists at leisure, talk to them, learn their tastes, and exploit opportunities to cater to their needs and desires.

3. Their language and culture are much closer to those of most tourists, and this facilitates mutual understanding. In the case of Mexico, a great many tourists speak enough Spanish to make at least rudimentary communication easy.

4. Many members of the local elite already control the capital, real estate, and other resources necessary to develop the infrastructure of services catering to tourists: hotels, restaurants, curio stores, travel agencies, buses and taxis, and the like.

5. Even the working class of the "national" group has an advantage compared to the touree in finding employment in the tourist industry, through greater ease of interaction with tourists. Thus, for instance, luxury restaurants and hotels prefer to hire mestizos as waiters, porters, and the like, even if they dress them up as Indians to make them more attractive to tourists.

TOURISTS, TOUREES, AND MIDDLEMEN

Basically, then, ethnic tourism creates a tripartite situation. It involves the interaction of tourists, tourees, and middlemen (van den Berghe 1980; van den Berghe and Keyes 1984). Ethnic tourism essentially superimposes itself on a preexisting system of ethnic relations wherein a locally dominant ethnic group, which represents the "national" culture and society, exerts its political, economic, and cultural control over one or more indigenous groups. The indigenes become the tourees while the "nationals" become the middlemen of the tourist industry. Third World elites act as intermediaries, bringing tourists and tourees together. The middlemen physically occupy the strategic towns where First, Third, and Fourth Worlds meet. They control the economic resources to provide the infrastructure of tourist services. Their own culture facilitates access to tourists. Their traditional power over the tourees enables them to control tourist access to tourees. Finally, their knowledge of both tourists and local conditions puts them in a privileged position to discover, create, and exploit the many new economic niches that proliferate with tourism, to manipulate indigenous cultural symbols for commercial gain (such as decorating hotels or restaurants with indigenous crafts), indeed, even to alter indigenous culture for tourist marketing (for example, by creating settings of "staged authenticity," such as "native dances," for tourist consumption).

While the middlemen are in an advantageous position to manipulate and market ethnicity for tourist consumption, they have by no means a monopoly of the trade. Tourees, too, modify their behavior and their cultural artifacts in response to tourist demand, and seek to derive economic benefits from literally making a spectacle of themselves. However, in most cases, their ability to control tourist access and to benefit from it is much more limited because of their subordinate position in the social order. There is also a wide range of individual and community reactions to tourism on the part of tourees. Some react mostly through avoidance (refusing, for instance, to be photographed), while others start producing and marketing "tourist art," putting themselves and their products on show in strategic tourist locations, such as outside hotels and restaurants.

Even tourists (or ex-tourists turned residents) get into the tourist business as producers of tourist goods (such as designer clothes incorporating local weavings), as purchasers of local handicrafts for resale abroad, as tour guides specializing in their own language group, as craftsmen selling their own wares in the tourist market, and so on. That is, a few tourists turn middlemen, as do a few tourees, but most middlemen are local townsmen, often of bourgeois origin, who are local members of the "national" culture.

Ethnic tourism is a uniquely interesting phenomenon for students of ethnic relations. First, the presence of tourists introduces a new dimension to preexisting systems of ethnic relations, such as existed in San Cristóbal between ladinos and Indians. At the most obvious and superficial level, tourists belong to many different ethnic groups, and interact with each other as well as with tourees and middlemen.

Second, the similar conditions, behavior, and interests of tourists are conducive to their being lumped together into a single category which acquires quasi-ethnic attributes expressed as stereotypes. Tourists become a transient super-ethny, merging into a temporary melting pot, only to resume their separate ethnic identities when they return home. In Jafari's (1987) terms, tourists leap out of their ordinary lives to enter temporarily a tourist culture operating in a ludic, non-ordinary world. Despite the ethnic tourists' often expressed resentment at the presence of other tourists who "spoil the natives," tourists do, in fact, interact a great deal with one another, to exchange information, but also for sociability. In the process, they constantly modify each other's behavior, destinations, purchases, and so on. They create, in short, a subculture of their own, which is ephemeral in their own existence, yet persistent in the localities they visit. The personnel change, but the subculture endures, as it is created by the intersection of the tourist's non-ordinary life with the host's ordinary life (Jafari 1987).

Third, while ethnic tourism superimposes itself on preexisting systems of ethnic relations, it does not leave the latter unaffected. It becomes, in fact, a powerful source of ethnic change in a number of complex ways. Tourism can lead to rapid economic development, which in turn can transform power relations between different class and ethnic groups. Tourism can alter gender relations (as when women market handicrafts they control, such as weaving or pottery, and thus gain greater economic independence). Tourism can accelerate processes of acculturation and assimilation of marginal groups into the "national" society (by fostering the introduction of new goods and services, the construction of access roads to remote villages, and so on). Conversely, however, the commercialization of ethnic exoticism and ethnic crafts can lead to the renaissance of native cultures, to the re-creation of ethnicity, or to the invention of new traditions that are neither "traditional" nor mainstream "modern" (Graburn 1976; MacCannell 1984; Popelka and Littrell 1991; van den Berghe and Keyes 1984).

The cultural content of these re-creations frequently changes, and indeed the ethnic boundaries themselves can change; but tourism can be, and frequently is, a stimulus for cultural creativity and innovation. Ethnic tourism not only debases and destroys what it touches, it also renews and transforms it in profoundly creative ways. The staged authenticity of tourist shows can sometimes become the authentic stage of a cultural revival (van den Berghe 1980). At the very least, one should suspend negative value judgments as to the impact of tourism on indigenous cultures. The processes of ethnic change unleashed by tourism are too varied and complex to be easily summarized by facile negative judgments, as shown, for instance, by Kottak's (1983) account of the impact of sun-sand-and-sea tourism in northeastern Brazil. Neither, of course, are Panglossian paeans to tourism as a "passport to development" and an "industry without smokestacks" appropriate summations of the effects of tourism (de Kadt 1979). Tourism is neither as good nor as bad as many people suppose, but much more complex and interesting than simple, categorical judgments can capture.[5]

Fourth, ethnic tourism possesses a number of characteristics and paradoxes that make its study especially fascinating. Ethnic tourism, insofar as it is a quest for the other, is plagued by a ubiquitous "Heisenberg effect": the observer affects the observed. The quest for authenticity is constantly threatened by the very interaction between tourist and touree (Cohen 1972, 1988; Riley 1988). Yet the interaction can also

5. The economic impact is, of course, uncontestable. In 1988, the World Tourism Organization estimated international tourist expenditures at $195 billion. In 1985, about $8.45 billion were spent on handicraft exports from developing countries. Handicrafts were estimated to be the second largest source of income in developing countries after agriculture. In Latin America alone, some 40 million people are involved in handicraft production (Popelka and Littrell 1991:393).

produce new culture forms that neither party anticipated. Ethnic tourism creates constantly shifting ethnic frontiers. Few ethnic situations are as fluid, dynamic, and productive of human creativity (Graburn 1976).

Let us now spell out the main characteristics which make tourist-host interactions such a special type of human relationship.

1. Tourist-host interactions are highly asymmetrical on two important dimensions that cut in opposite ways. First, tourists frequently have higher status than their hosts, if only because they can afford to be there. This is especially true of First World tourism in Third World countries, but is also obvious in much internal tourism within rich countries. Even the seemingly "poor" counterculture tourist on a shoestring budget enjoys the enormous luxury of leisure. This is obviously not to say that all tourists are wealthier than all locals, but nearly all tourist-host interaction takes the form of an unequal relationship between consumers of sights, spectacles, and services, and those who provide these commodities either simply by being there, by making a spectacle of themselves, or by making a living from tourism. Egalitarian interaction between tourist and host is rare. Second, there is a great asymmetry of useful knowledge between tourists and hosts, and one which cuts in the opposite direction to that of status. The host has the great advantage of being on home turf, and thus knowledgeable of local conditions, prices, sights, services, and so on. That knowledge, pitched against tourist ignorance, can be turned to profit. The tourist, on the other hand, faces the option of either learning fast or being "taken." The burden on tourists of having to learn the local ropes fast is only imperfectly lessened by guidebooks and is often aggravated by language barriers.

2. Tourist-host interactions are ephemeral and unlikely to be repeated, and thus are especially open to mistrust, cheating, and broken contracts. Tourists so much expect to be "taken" that they frequently express surprise when they are not (for example, when the swimming pool promised in a hotel brochure actually turns out to contain water on arrival). Conversely, natives are pleasantly surprised when they actually receive a print of the promised photograph of themselves. Both sides have limited expectations of each other where immediacy of the exchange is considered the best substitute for nonexisting trust.

Ethnic tourism thus creates situations which maximize mutual misunderstanding and exploitation, irrespective of the participants' intentions. Ideally (from the perspective of the tourist), tourist and touree are "perfect strangers" to one another. The very transience of their interaction means that neither will have the time to know the other, even if one of them should feel inclined to make the effort. For most ethnic tourists, the quest for the other becomes a mental file of ethnic vignettes, a vast kaleidoscope of cultural exotica, periodically reexperienced through slide shows. Ethnic tourism is a kind of caricature of ethnography, and thus a salutary inducement for the anthropologist to be self-critically introspective. Transience not only maximizes misunderstanding, it also fosters cheating and exploitation. The low probability of repeated interaction means that bad behavior goes unpunished. Both tourists and tourees frequently have good reason to feel abused and shortchanged—symbolically, verbally, or physically. Tourists feel cheated in the purchase of goods and services. Tourees feel intruded upon in their sense of privacy, underpaid for their goods or services, or humiliated by discourtesy. Yet, to the extent that relations continue to be actively sought, rewards presumably exceed punishments.[6]

3. Tourist-host interactions are segmented and instrumental: they are entered into for specific, limited, and immediate purposes, and they are not expected to have far-reaching or long-lasting consequences. When they blossom into friendship, this is considered exceptional and atypical.

4. Tourist-host interactions are especially vulnerable to faulty communication and misunderstandings, because they are often conducted across wide linguistic and cultural barriers, and in the absence of mutually understood norms and expectations on such delicate matters as etiquette of politeness, standards of privacy, and the like.

5. Like other forms of relations between different class, ethnic, or racial groups, tourist-host interactions often take place within the framework of crude stereotypes which each side has of the other. In the absence of both the time and the incentive to develop more individu-

6. For an extraordinarily vivid account of tourist-touree interactions under conditions approximating maximum feasible misunderstanding, see the film *Cannibal Tours* (O'Rourke 1987), and analyses of it (Bruner 1989; Lutkehaus 1989; MacCannell 1992).

alized, nuanced, and complex relationships, both sides find it expedient to draw caricatures of each other.

6. In spite of all these properties that would seem to doom tourist-host interaction to a perpetual state of friction and conflict, these interactions are typically found to be profitable and even enjoyable enough to be continued, because mutual expectations are low and because the interactions are carefully bracketed in both time and space. Neither side allows them to spill into "normal life," the tourist by removing himself from the situation whenever he chooses, the host by corralling tourists in narrow spatial enclaves. (Tourist hotels, restaurants, and sights typically contain 90 percent or more of tourists within one percent or less of the national territory.) Tourist segregation in gilded ghettos seems to be a mutually satisfying solution in many situations. Both tourists and hosts frequently keep each other at a carefully measured arm's length. (For example, tourist health phobias impede native friendship and hospitality, while, conversely, native disapproval of public nudity, drinking, and lovemaking is accommodated by high walls around luxury hotels.) Mutual avoidance, except within well-defined situations motivated by curiosity (on the tourist side) and material interest (on the host side), is often a satisfactory modus vivendi.

Some of the features listed above are not exclusive to ethnic tourism. However, ethnic tourism, in part because of the very special clientele it attracts, is probably the most culturally complex and interesting to study. It creates the most dynamic types of ethnic relations that highlight, in accelerated and exaggerated form, processes also present in other forms of tourism, or in other forms of ethnic relations. Perhaps as a special case of both tourism and ethnic relations, ethnic tourism accentuates the most interesting features of both. Its study is guaranteed to satisfy even the most inquisitive and imaginative scholars, and to disabuse them of any notion that tourism is a trivial phenomenon.

THE INTERFACE OF

ANTHROPOLOGY AND

TOURISM

2   METHODOLOGY

    At one level, all anthropology is autobiography. The field-work for this study took place between January and March of 1990, a relatively short time by the standards of ethnographic research. However, I have known and studied the town of San Cristóbal since 1959, when I accompanied Evon Vogt, Benjamin (Nick) Colby, and Lore Colby as the first research team of the Harvard Chiapas Project. Nick Colby and I then studied ethnic relations in the area, he from the perspective of Zinacanteco Indians, and I from the ladino side of the ethnic boundary in the town of San Cristóbal (Colby 1966; Colby and van den Berghe 1961; van den Berghe and Colby 1961). Since that time, I have made periodic visits to San Cristóbal and environs: in 1966, when

I collaborated with Colby again on a study of ethnic relations among the Ixil of Quiché Department, Guatemala (Colby and van den Berghe 1969); in 1972, on my way to Cuzco for another study of ethnic relations in the southern Andes of Peru (van den Berghe and Primov 1977); in 1977, as part of another Mexican trip; and in 1987, when I revisited both the Ixil area and the Chiapas highlands.

The choice of San Cristóbal as the setting of this study is thus anything but accidental. It resulted from three decades of work in the area, and a continuing interest in ethnic relations. The connection between ethnicity and tourism may not be obvious, but I see at least three essential points of overlap:

1. The type of tourism that I am especially interested in is *ethnic tourism*: the tourism in which the exotic culture of the "touree" is the tourist's principal attractant.

2. The tourist, being by definition a stranger, creates by his very presence a situation of ethnic relations.

3. In situations of ethnic tourism, the tourist frequently comes to see marginal, Fourth World indigenes of host societies which are dominated by groups less exotic to the tourist. Thus the tourist's presence both complicates and modifies a preexisting system of ethnic relations which now include tourists, indigenes (whom I termed "tourees"), and the local representatives of the dominant "national" culture (van den Berghe and Keyes 1984).

My interest in ethnic tourism was first awakened during my 1972-73 Peruvian fieldwork (van den Berghe and Primov 1977; van den Berghe 1980), but that study was much broader in scope and was not specifically focused on tourism. The present work is my first piece of fieldwork centering exclusively on tourism, and, to my knowledge, the first book-length ethnography of tourism in a Mexican town. (See, however, Brewer 1984, for an article on stereotypes of tourists in San Felipe, Baja California Norte, and Kemper, 1978, 1981, for accounts of tourism in Pátzcuaro, Michoacán.) The idea of studying tourism in San Cristóbal came to me during my 1987 visit. A tight schedule prevented me from doing the research then, but it was strikingly obvious that San Cristóbal had undergone an explosion in the volume of tourist traffic between my last two visits (1977 and 1987). In one decade, the town had moved from a small daily volume of scores of mostly backpack tourists to a daily flow of hundreds of tourists of all descriptions, including several busloads of organized tour customers. It was equally clear to me that the town was being profoundly affected in the process, and thus offered a prime opportunity for the study of many fascinating social phenomena brought about by the tourist presence.

I make no claim that San Cristóbal represents, in any sense, a typical tourist situation, although it probably shares a number of characteristics with other provincial Third World cities that serve as regional market towns for surrounding Fourth World peoples (like, say, Cuzco, Peru, or Chiang Mai, Thailand), and thus become magnets of ethnic tourism. My interest in San Cristóbal, however, was more in its idiosyncrasy than in its problematic typicality.

In many ways, this study was the easiest, most pleasant, and most unproblematic piece of fieldwork I ever conducted. Being self-funded (except for a sabbatical leave from the University of Washington), I was not burdened by the tedium of grant administration, fettered by the strings of outside sponsorship, or exposed to the kind of obscurantist attack which my Peruvian research attracted (van den Berghe 1989). (Senator William Proxmire gave me a Golden Fleece Award for it, and the present study was an equally attractive candidate. In the eyes of a backwoods politico, a study of tourism must look like the ultimate boondoggle.)

My long-standing friendship and collaboration with a number of local people made research access unproblematic. With the exception of one tourist guide who refused me an interview after breaking two appointments, all local people extended to me their enthusiastic collaboration and, in many cases, their warm friendship and hospitality as well. (The one exception was a young woman who specializes in taking small groups of English-speaking tourists for "unusual tours" of the two neighboring Indian communities of Zinacantán and Chamula. She felt threatened by my expertise as an anthropologist, and probably feared that I might expose the limits of her claimed expertise on the Indian villages she was marketing to tourists.)

Besides the general friendliness of San Cristóbal people, the town offers a stimulating milieu in which to work, with a sizable local intelligentsia of people highly knowledgeable about the town and the region: Mexican and foreign historians, archaeologists, anthropologists, and others teach at local schools and faculties of the University of Chiapas, work in several locally based federal research institutes, offices (such as the Instituto Nacional Indígenista) or museums, or do field research. The books of several resident authors are available in local bookstores, and at least eight or ten sizable libraries in private homes, museums, research institutes, or government offices are available to local scholars. Public lectures on history or archaeology, and showings of ethnographic or foreign art films, are almost daily events. San Cristóbal, in short, is no longer a cultural backwater.

Finally, Mexico as a whole provides a climate of almost unlimited freedom to engage in intellectual debate and conduct scientific research (subject to some restrictions in the field of archaeology, out of a legitimate concern for the integrity of sites and the possible misappropriation of artifacts). Those familiar with fieldwork conditions in Latin America, Africa, or Asia know how exceptional is Mexico's unfettered freedom to do research. Indeed, I encountered more difficulties doing research on my own campus (especially from the petty bureaucracy of the Human Subjects Review Committee) than I have in Mexico.

Like most ethnographic studies, this one relied primarily on interviews and participant observation as sources of data, supplemented by available archival sources. By far the most important source of already collected data came from the local Oficina de Turismo, of the state of Chiapas tourism promotion bureau, where the two employees, Magdalena Mandujano Santiago and Lucía Méndez Toporek, cheerfully put their extremely useful statistical records at my disposal.

The most systematic interview data came from a nonrandom sample of 175 tourists to whom I administered a short, one-page semistructured schedule, which could be completed in about ten minutes for the hurried tourists afraid to fall behind their conducted tour. In at least 95 percent of the cases, however, the individual interview lasted much longer, averaging perhaps thirty to forty minutes. In some 25 percent of the cases, the interview extended to an hour, and in a dozen or so cases it developed into several hours of conversation, interaction, and observation, including shared trips and meals. In perhaps twenty or twenty-five cases, I met the same tourists on successive days, and followed up on my initial interview, filling in details of their experiences. In some 80 percent of my tourist interviews, the prepared schedule merely served as a semiformal introduction to a much longer, unstructured, and freer conversation, in which I also offered to reciprocate by answering questions tourists might want to ask of me. Besides giving me the opportunity to offer a valuable commodity to tourists (reliable knowledge about local conditions, sites, schedules, and the like) in return for their cooperation, their questions were, of course, highly revealing of their interests, concerns, and anxieties. Tourists also had an opportunity to check my information against that given to them by guidebooks, other tourists, and local people, and thus they indirectly gave me insights into tourist modes of gathering information.

The choice of whom to interview was obviously not random. It was first filtered through my notion of who was a tourist, by no means as straightforward a definitional question as might appear (Cohen 1974). Many tourists are clearly identifiable as foreigners, but I was also interested in sampling Mexican tourists. Furthermore, not all obvious foreigners are tourists, as San Cristóbal hosts a community of about eighty to one hundred long-term resident gringos who would resent the label of tourist. At one end of the spectrum, the definitional problem is minimal: the camera-toting person moving in a monolingual phalanx under the guidance of a lecturing *cicerone*, and boarding a special luxury bus labeled "Turismo" presents no taxonomic problem. But how about the long-haired, barefoot, raggedly dressed, "spaced-out" young man meditating in the sun on a Zócalo bench? (One such described himself as a "pilgrim" in response to the question about his occupation.) Several of the people whom I had picked as tourists for my sample spontaneously rejected the label, and preferred to call themselves "travelers." There was some obvious disparity between my definition and the view some of my respondents had of themselves. Yet, even the self-styled "travelers" accepted the *role* of tourist if not the word, and did not object to being part of my definition of a study of tourism.

Specifically, what criteria of inclusion did I use in defining a person as a tourist? Typically, a candidate for inclusion had to satisfy three or more of the following characteristics:

1. Being phenotypically not Indian or mestizo looking.
2. Speaking a language other than Spanish or a local Mayan language.

3. Being obviously not an Indian, as determined mostly by clothing and language.
4. Taking photographs and carrying photographic equipment.
5. Speaking poor, accented, incorrect Spanish (except if Indian).
6. Showing an interest in "touristy" sights, or being in places catering primarily to tourists, such as craft markets and stores, hotels, restaurants, and cafés.
7. Looking lost, asking for directions, showing ignorance of prices, appearing anxious, disconcerted, or puzzled.
8. Moving with a group of persons showing one or more of the above characteristics, except in the capacity of guide.
9. Following a guide or reading a guidebook.
10. Looking Mexican but not local, by exhibiting characteristics 3, 4, 6, 7, 8 or 9. (Mexican tourists, on the whole, looked and behaved less "touristy" than foreigners, however.)
11. Dressing "touristy," especially displaying newly acquired artifacts such as handwoven clothing and handbags.

In the overwhelming majority of cases, the attribution of tourist status was easy, instantaneous, consensual, and unambiguous. The definitional problems arose only in the rare deviant cases, not in the modal ones.

If transience is part of the definition of the tourist, there is also the question of how long it takes for a tourist to become a resident? Over 60 percent of my sample had spent more than a month in Mexico; 14 percent, more than three months. Many clearly fit the profile of the long-term, low-budget tourist (Riley 1988). Even though I consciously avoided including the resident gringos (drawing the arbitrary line at six months continuous stay in San Cristóbal), my sample included two persons who had been in San Cristóbal over three months.

Local gainful employment did not necessarily exclude one from the sample. A number of young counterculture, backpack tourists earned travel money by hawking costume jewelry to other tourists or playing music in restaurants, thus straddling both sides of the tourism fence. They were both tourists and providers of tourist services.

Notwithstanding all these interesting problems of objective and subjective definitions, my sample includes only one person who probably does not fit the category of tourist in the sense of a nonlocal person who travels principally for pleasure. He was a young man from a neighboring small town whom I caught "behaving like a tourist"; that is, he was slowly inspecting the wares offered by Indian vendors of tourist textiles. It turned out that he was killing time, having driven his father to town for a medical checkup. But since I had taken him for a tourist, I left him in the sample. No doubt, I consciously or unconsciously excluded a number of persons whose status as tourists was similarly marginal. For instance, I approached a group of young Mexican men dressed in ponchos (a very touristy thing to do), bargaining with Indian vendors, but decided against interviewing any of them when I found out they were soldiers from the locally garrisoned infantry battalion. Yet, the young man I was about to interview proudly identified himself as coming from Guanajuato, a distant city of central Mexico, and clearly sought to establish himself as a nonlocal.

Most of the tourists I interviewed were approached in a few locations in central San Cristóbal (see Map 2). My favorite interviewing ground was the craft market of Santo Domingo. Practically every tourist went through it, usually at a fairly leisurely pace, shopping for textiles and other made-for-tourists artifacts. I also liked it because the area was open and an ideal field of observation, giving me opportunities to select my informants and observe them before interviewing them, and because a row of stone benches on the outer rim of the market provided a comfortable setting for the interviews. Perhaps a third of the sample was interviewed in that market, with possibly a slight bias toward buyers of artifacts. The remaining two-thirds or so of the sample were approached in a variety of locales: in the tourist office when they came in for information (with a bias toward the most recently arrived); while resting on a Zócalo bench (a comfortable setting in an unhurried situation); in restaurants (after they had finished their meal); in hotel lobbies; in outlying Indian villages, mostly in Chamula; in buses or in bus stations while waiting for their bus.

When unable to guess the nationality, I would ask the prospective respondent in English what his or her nationality was, and then shift to one of the four languages in which I am fluent (French, Spanish, German, or English) to match the respondent's mother tongue (which I was able to do in 89 percent of the cases) or at least his or her best second language. For Italian, Japanese, and Brazilian tourists, the best second language was generally Spanish; for most other nationalities, English. I would then state: "I am an anthropologist doing a study on the impact of tourism here in San Cristóbal. I would like to ask you a few questions. Do you have ten or fifteen minutes?" One American man turned me down categorically, stating almost belligerently: "I don't want to be part of any survey on any subject." Some eight to ten other people, usually traveling in tour groups and afraid of missing their bus or falling behind the rest of the group, courteously declined to be interviewed, pleading lack of time. This translates into a refusal rate of approximately 5 to 6 percent (10 out of 185). Even if one adds to them the half-dozen interviews out of the 175 in the sample which were given somewhat reluctantly or hurriedly and yielded somewhat truncated data, over 90 percent of all the attempted interviews were satisfactorily completed.

While the choice of respondents was not random, I consciously sought to achieve both representativeness and diversity in gender, age, nationality, social class, mode of transport, and style of travel. For instance, when interviewing respondents who were traveling as couples, I tried to interview an approximately equal number of men and women. However, men are somewhat overrepresented because the husband frequently asserted himself as the person to be interviewed or "stole" the interview away from his wife. Travel companions were often present during interviews, and frequently volunteered comments. I did nothing to discourage such interjections, since I wanted to keep the situation as easy and free-flowing as possible. But I always kept the focus on the person interviewed and identified separately the comments of the other person. On a handful of occasions, when the other person, usually a man, "stole" the interview from his companion early in the interview, I shifted the focus person to the interjector when it had become clear that he had de facto become the respondent.

I undersampled Mexican tourists, because of their lower phenotypic visibility, and organized-group tourists because their hurried and harried look discouraged approach. Otherwise, my sample does not greatly deviate in profile from the tourist office statistics. These statistics themselves, however, are biased in the direction of people who spend at least one night in a San Cristóbal hotel or pension, and thus undersample the very transient (who spend less than a day in town), the young and parsimonious who camp or sleep in cheap, unlisted accommodations, and Mexicans who stay with friends and relatives. My sample probably includes more of the long-term, "shoestring" tourists and fewer of the organized tour variety than the official statistics.

Besides interviewing tourists, I also interviewed, though less formally and systematically, most hotel and pension owners or managers, many restaurant keepers, and a number of travel agents, taxi drivers, tourist shopkeepers, travel guides, teachers, tourist-office workers, street vendors and hawkers, shoeshine boys, waiters, weavers—in short, a wide range of ladinos and Indians who come into contact with tourists. All of them, numbering well over a hundred persons, were interviewed in Spanish, as I have no knowledge of either of the two main Maya languages spoken in the vicinity of San Cristóbal: Tzotzil and Tzeltal. Most of the Indians who come in contact with tourists now have a fairly good utilitarian command of Spanish, though seldom enough to express subtle and complex thoughts. My study thus cannot claim to have captured at any depth Indian attitudes toward tourists.

Interviewing is only one side of anthropological fieldwork. Participant observation is the other. This technique is peculiarly well suited to a study of tourism. Without even trying, I found it extremely easy to be taken for a tourist myself, especially as I was making extensive use of my camera to record tourist behavior and interactions with natives. I lived in a hotel near the Zócalo, took most of my meals in the score or so of restaurants frequented by tourists, joined tourist groups on buses, and observed them quite unobtrusively in markets, hotels, restaurants, buses, shops, churches, museums—indeed the entire range of public places they frequented. In fact, only when I explicitly introduced myself as an anthropologist doing research was my cover "blown," and then only to the people I addressed. The very transience of tourists added to the ease of my participant observation. The few people in the know would be gone within days.

In effect, only a small set of close San Cristóbal friends and acquaintances, both Mexican and foreign, were fully aware of my presence as a social scientist, and few of them were involved in the study. Perhaps the best measure of my successful participation in the tourist scene was that most Indian street vendors and hawkers continued to treat me as a

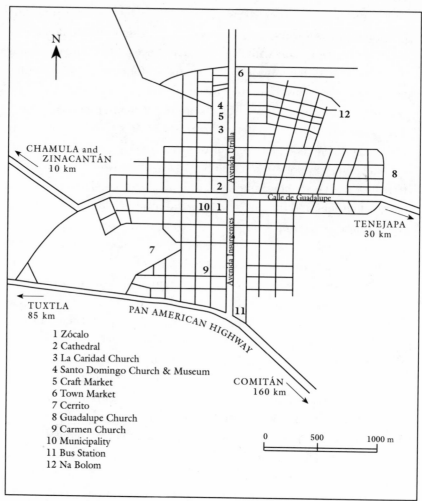

N

CHAMULA and
ZINACANTÁN
10 km

Avenida Utrilla

Avenida Insurgentes

Calle de Guadalupe

TENEJAPA
30 km

TUXTLA
85 km

PAN AMERICAN HIGHWAY

COMITÁN
160 km

1 Zócalo
2 Cathedral
3 La Caridad Church
4 Santo Domingo Church & Museum
5 Craft Market
6 Town Market
7 Cerrito
8 Guadalupe Church
9 Carmen Church
10 Municipality
11 Bus Station
12 Na Bolom

0   500   1000 m

Map 2. San Cristóbal

tourist and to proffer their wares for sale, week after week. (A couple of observant Chamula young women in the Santo Domingo market, however, did notice my interviewing and note-taking, and realized that I was not a tourist, at least not in the conventional sense.)

Several of the resident gringos knew what I was doing, but most tourists were too busy observing to notice that they were under observation. Sometimes, I would follow a tourist group closely enough to be within earshot of normal conversation, for a period of half an hour or more, without anyone displaying any consciousness of being observed. This was true even though I was not attempting to conceal my note-taking, and would sometimes stand next to a tourist for a five- to ten-minute bargaining session. Being themselves an object of curiosity is not a conscious part of the tourist experience. Indeed, when I would reveal the subject of my research to prospective respondents, several reacted with great amusement to the suggestion that as tourists they were, in effect, becoming the anthropologist's natives. Nevertheless, tourists *are* clearly being observed, not only by inquisitive anthropologists but by ordinary townsmen to whom they offer a considerable source of entertainment. The average tourist is too absorbed in his own voyeurism of natives to realize that the curiosity is mutual, although one particularly insightful tourist remarked to me that this must be the case.

Participant observation of tourist-host interactions was made even easier because the overwhelming bulk of such interactions took place in a circumscribed area: the two markets, the Zócalo, and the bus stations, connected by a street some 1.8 kilometers long. Nearly all the tourist hotels and restaurants are located within two blocks (about 200 meters) of that street and along three blocks of two intersecting streets that lead to the Zócalo. The most distant "points of interest" in tourist San Cristóbal are within fifteen-minute walk of the Zócalo; most are no more than five minutes away. Tourists, in fact, use taxis and the public transportation system (mostly microbuses called *colectivos*) much less frequently than locals. Without trying, I saw the same tourists up to three or four times a day, even though the total number of tourists in town on any given day averaged between 600 and 800. It was thus easy to observe the same individuals in a variety of situations (such as bargaining with Chamula Indians in the marketplace, visiting a museum or church, eating lunch, conversing with other tourists on the Zócalo, or asking for maps or directions in the tourist office).

Finally, I should mention one more fact of my participant observation in San Cristóbal, which was less directly connected with my research, but was nevertheless significant. Both through old and new acquaintances, I became integrated in the small local intelligentsia. I visited a number of historians, linguists, anthropologists, archaeologists, and others, both at their homes and in their research institutes or offices. I was invited to give talks (one of them to the students of a vocational school training tourist guides and hotel managers). This was another minor way of reciprocating the town's hospitality. One of these talks was publicized over the radio, delivered in the auditorium of the large historical museum, and attended by well over a hundred people—much of San Cristóbal's intellectual elite. Four days later, as I was buying my *Excelsior* at the bookstore next to my hotel, a young man approached me with a four-page typescript of notes of my lecture, asking that I check it for accuracy. In fact, I also discovered that some of my works were being read in Spanish translation by students at the local social sciences faculty of the University of Chiapas, and that my previous work in the region (and its critique by the well-known Mexican sociologist, Rodolfo Stavenhagen) was part of the intellectual discourse of local social scientists. The son of another eminent Mexican sociologist, Pablo González Casanova, a physician with the same name, lives in San Cristóbal, is well acquainted with my work, invited me to give a talk to his institute for ecological research, and became a friend. It turned out that his wife was the owner of the hotel where I stayed, and my name in the hotel registry first made him aware of my presence in town.

In short, my fieldwork in San Cristóbal was totally free of the many problems and crises which affected nearly all of my other field experiences. As many of my colleagues have suspected all along, it came closest to what might be called a working vacation, a totally pleasurable experience in a stimulating environment, where I could bask in the friendly hospitality and companionship of both friends and strangers. Perhaps I have discovered anthropological Nirvana, by becoming one with my subject, the anthropologist cum tourist. In the end, what is anthropology but the ultimate form of ethnic tourism, the endless quest for self-understanding through the exotic other?

ETHNIC AND

CLASS RELATIONS

IN SAN CRISTÓBAL

AND THE

DEVELOPMENT

OF TOURISM

3   THE SETTING

In the last three decades, San Cristóbal has grown from a
dormant provincial town of some 20,000 to a vibrant small city of
over 100,000. During my first visit in 1959, the recently paved Pan-
American Highway had reached the Guatemalan border and was beginning to bring a trickle of adventuresome North American motorists
on their way to Central America. From San Cristóbal, a car could only
travel east to Guatemala or west to Tuxtla, the state capital of Chiapas
(See Map 1). In this extreme southeastern periphery of Mexico, San
Cristóbal was a small market town in a poor, isolated rural highland
area known for its Indians. In the Mexican worldview of the day, this
was synonymous with backwardness.

Indeed, backward was the direction toward which the local elite turned their gaze. In relative terms, San Cristóbal had known somewhat more prominence in colonial days than during the independence period. Cuidad Real de Chiapa had been a bishopric since the mid-sixteenth century, and it was a significant religious and commercial center on the dorsal spine of the Vice-Royalty of New Spain, a way station linking the larger highland colonial cities to the northwest (Oaxaca, Puebla, and Mexico) to the Captaincy General of Guatemala. The 1778 census gave San Cristóbal a population of 4,814, living in 586 houses, 136 of them with tile roofs, 450 with straw roofs (de Vos 1986:25). Around it were six Indian barrios. The town center, built in the standard Spanish grid pattern around a Plaza Mayor, was graced with a handful of large convents and a few blocks of large adobe mansions. Many of these sixteenth, seventeenth, and eighteenth century buildings survive to this day (figs. 3, 4).

San Cristóbal was at the heart of a densely populated Indian area. Indians meant tribute payments and labor, and these in turn could support a sizable parasitic class of Spanish clergy, officials, and landowners, and a middle class of mestizo merchants, artisans, and muleteers. San Cristóbal was a rigid, tight little society stratified into racial *castas*, ruled tyrannically by a double hierarchy of clergy and lay officials, and milked rapaciously for tribute by its dominant Spanish stratum. Every Indian between eighteen and fifty had to pay, in money or produce, two pesos a year, a considerable sum then for impoverished subsistence peasants (de Vos 1986:47).

The 1778 census listed 564 Spaniards (most of them probably American-born criollos), 1,882 mestizos (predominantly a petite bourgeoisie of small merchants, craftsmen, and muleteers, but also drifters and hangers-on of the upper class), 830 blacks and mulatoes (both slaves and freedmen, but many of them skilled workers and house servants, for blacks were expensive compared to Indians, who did not have to be bought), and 2,115 Indians (who occupied the broad base of the social pyramid as peasants and unskilled workers). The total of 5,391 included the six Indian barrios (de Vos 1986:73–74), but not the much larger hinterland population of more distant Indian pueblos.

Independence, declared in 1810 but not effectively exercised until 1821, changed little in local relations of power and of production. Power was transferred to the criollos and wealthy mestizos, who, in any case, had already been rising economically and politically during the Bourbon monarchy, and black slaves were freed, but the Indian peasantry remained at the bottom of the social structure. The first half of the nineteenth century was a period of political turmoil characterized by a large degree of both economic stagnation and local autonomy of regional elites due to geographical isolation and a weak, ineffective central government. The power of the Church, however, was weakened by various waves of secularization and expropriation, culminating in Juárez's Reform Laws.

San Cristóbal became, if anything, even more of a backwater in the nineteenth century than during the colonial era. Even the period of economic expansion and modernization of the Porfiriato (1884–1910), based on railroad construction, mining, and export agriculture on large haciendas, left San Cristóbal behind. Its mountainous hinterland of small-scale peasant holdings produced little surplus beyond feeding the local towns. The difficult terrain discouraged railway construction, which hugged to coastal lowlands, and left highland Chiapas isolated until the motorcar became part of the local scene in the 1920s and 1930s. Even then, dirt roads were extremely rudimentary. Indeed, mule transport and human porterage continued to dominate the traffic between Indian villages and San Cristóbal until the 1960s, when access roads to remote villages were finally built.

Except for the impoverishment of the Church due to expropriations and even religious persecution in the 1920s, the local power and economic structure in highland Chiapas was substantially unaffected until the mid-twentieth century. Ladinos remained firmly in control of both the economy and local government.

The ladino town of San Cristóbal lived parasitically on its Indian hinterland, which fed it. Ladinos and Indians lived side by side in an uneasy patron-client relationship based on mutual dependence, social inequality, political domination, and economic exploitation. Ladinos depended on Indians for labor and food, which they extracted by controlling the government machinery, the social services (schools, medical services), and the entire urban market and distribution system, including the manufactured products that Indians had come to rely on as necessities. These ties of dependence and domination were reinforced by personal links of *compadrazgo* (ritual kinship established around the Catholic sacraments of baptism, confirmation, and marriage) between ladino patrons and Indian clients (Colby 1966; Colby and van den Berghe 1961).

In the ladino upper class, relations with Indians tended to take a more paternalistic form, as powerful, wealthy ladinos were chosen by Indians as godparents of their children, thus establishing patron-client ties across ethnic lines. These ties often developed into economic and domestic relationships as well. For example, Indian goddaughters would come to work as maids in ladino households. Among the ladino working class or petite bourgeoisie, however, relations to Indians were more competitive and even openly hostile. Not infrequently, ladinos would insult Indians or push them aside on the marketplace (behavior I observed only once during my 1990 fieldwork).

Ladinos of all social classes looked down on Indians as backward, addicted to alcohol, ignorant, uncivilized, and dirty, though they also regarded them as good, hard-working peasants. A clear etiquette of inequality marked social distance between ladinos and Indians. For instance, ladinos spoke to Indians as they would to children of their own group, denying them courtesy titles such as "Don" or "Señor," using the familiar "tu" form, and referring to Indian adults as *inditos* or *muchachos*, irrespective of age. They expected Indians, on the other hand, to behave deferentially toward them.

The Chiapas highlands were, in short, a plural society stratified by social class and segmented by ethnicity. The ladinos lived overwhelmingly in the town of San Cristóbal, though a sprinkling of ladinos also lived in outlying Indian communities as teachers, petty officials, and traders (figs. 6, 7, 8, 9). They controlled all levels of government, the police, the army, the courts, the schools, the clinics and hospitals, indeed, the entire public sector except for the municipal councils of the Indian villages. They also monopolized retail and wholesale trade, motor transport, the purchase and distribution of agricultural produce, and the hiring of migratory labor for the large estates. The ladinos were

an urban group, ranging from working class to ruling elite, and occupy-
ing nearly all positions and occupations in the social, political, and
economic structure at all levels above that of the local peasant village.
All ladinos shared Spanish as the "national" language, and were almost
invariably monolingual in Spanish, which they exclusively used as a
home language, as the official medium in schools and in government,
and as the language of the marketplace.

Indians, on the other hand, were both the bottom peasant stratum of a
society rigidly hierarchized by social class—by differential relations of
power and production—and a set of micronations with separate ethnic
identities (figs. 10, 11, 12, 13, 14). The Indians were internally un-
stratified by class, but differentiated, not only from the ladinos, but also
from each other, by language, style of dress, and many other cultural
markers. While, collectively, Indians were a peasantry in a stratified
class order, the local Indian communities were internally fairly classless
and differentiated only by individual gradation of wealth, influence,
and prestige. The village community was ruled by a male gerontocracy.
Individuals could accumulate wealth, but a decentralized political system and wealth redistribution linked with the holding of annual *cargos*
ensured a village society stratified primarily by age and gender rather
than by social class (Cancian 1965; Vogt 1966, 1970). Each village
community (*municipio*) constituted a microsociety clearly distinct, not
only from the "national" ladino society but also from other Indian
municipios, by clear ethnic markers, the most visible one being style of
dress, but also by language, dialect, and a number of local traditions,
fiestas, myths, beliefs, and so on.

Depending on whether one chooses to stress social class as an ana-
lytic tool (as most Latin American social scientists have tried to do) or
ethnicity (as have a number of North American scholars, myself included), one arrives at a slightly different interpretative account of the
local system of inequality in the distribution of power and wealth. This
has given rise to much intellectual debate (Benjamin 1989; Favre 1973,
1985; Wasserstrom 1983), including that over the work of Colby and
myself on San Cristóbal (Colby and van den Berghe 1961; van den
Berghe and Colby 1961; Goldkind 1963; Colby and van den Berghe
1964; Stavenhagen 1964; Colby and van den Berghe 1965). I have
always felt that the controversy is sterile. We deal obviously with *both*

class and ethnicity; neither is reducible to the other, because each constitutes a different basis of social organization (van den Berghe 1981). At one level, Indians are integrated politically and economically into a single class-stratified society where they occupy the bottom rung as a peasantry. At another level, the fifty-six Indian groups of Mexico are an ethnic archipelago scattered as the marginal remnants of conquered nations among a Spanish-speaking, dominant mestizo nation. Because they are linguistically and culturally differentiated from the mainstream of the Mexican nation, Indians are in a fundamentally distinct (and more marginal and subordinate) relationship to the dominant order than Spanish-speaking mestizo peasants. In short, the subordination and marginalization of Indians can be fully understood only if one takes into account that they are *both* Indians *and* peasants.

One final remark on the Mexican social order, and on the Chiapas highlands in particular, is perhaps obvious to Mexicans, but needs nonetheless to be stressed for other readers. The distinction between Indians and ladinos (or mestizos in the rest of Mexico) is *not* a racial or phenotypic one. Most ladinos or mestizos are physically undistinguishable from Indians. Perhaps 85 percent of the Mexican population are of predominantly Amerindian genetic stock, some 10 percent of African origin, and a bare 5 percent of European stock. The overwhelmingly dominant phenotype is Amerindian among both Indians and mestizos. Language and culture now define the distinction, not physical appearance. If one is a native speaker of an indigenous language, one is an Indian; if one's native tongue is Spanish, one is a ladino or mestizo. In colonial times, the terms "Indian" and "mestizo" were racial, but the labels have lost nearly all racial content in the last two centuries. In fact, in modern Mexican Spanish, the term *indio* has acquired a pejorative connotation, and the nonracial term *indígena* is the preferred, neutral one.

To be sure, members of the social elite of San Cristóbal are *disproportionately* lighter skinned and taller than most Indians (but also than most ladinos). Nonetheless, the ladinos, and even the upper class, cannot be described as "whites," because many could easily pass for Indians if they changed their dress and behavior. Conversely, there are a few light-skinned, gray-eyed, brown-haired Indians who clearly have European ancestry, and yet are defined as Indians. If anything, phenotype is a better predictor of class status among ladinos than of ethnicity, but most Mexicans of all social classes are Amerindian looking, except in the top elite.

Thus Indians can and do become ladinos or mestizos by learning Spanish and acculturating to the dominant culture. The process is gradual and is usually achieved by young individuals in their second and third decade of life. In the case of entire communities, it can take two or more generations. The usual transition from Indian to mestizo status is one of language. An individual or community gradually shifts from indigenous monolingualism to bilingualism, to Spanish dominance, to Spanish monolingualism.

TRANSFORMATIONS SINCE 1950

The midcentury is a convenient point from which to measure recent changes. It marks, if not the beginning, at least the acceleration of a number of trends which profoundly affected the regional society of highland Chiapas. Perhaps the most obvious of these is population increase. In the last decades, Mexico as a whole—Chiapas even more so—has been in the middle phase of its "demographic transition." A combination of continued high birth rates and plummeting death rates led to a population explosion of close to 3 percent per annum. The recent growth rate in the Indian areas was even higher than the national average as the full impact of improved access, education, sanitation, and public health was felt only in recent decades, and as birth rates have not yet begun to declines as they are doing in the more developed parts of the country.

Mexican cities grew even faster than the rural population, through a process of internal migration. Chiapas was less affected by rapid urbanization than the rest of the country, especially in the highlands, which are still largely rural. The highland towns, San Cristóbal and Comitán, grew more slowly than Tuxtla, the state capital, and Tapachula, a bustling coastal town, because the highlands are virtually devoid of secondary industry, mining, or even large-scale commercial agriculture. Highland towns are mostly trading and transportation centers serving a peasant population. Nonetheless, San Cristóbal grew from a population of 17,500 in 1950, to 25,700 in 1970, to 61,100 in 1980. These census figures are generally thought to be undercounts. A sign at the entrance of town gives the population as 89,000. An official state of Chiapas map, dated 1986, puts the population of the municipio of San Cristóbal at 82,221 in an area of 484 square kilometers, for a density of 170 inhabitants per square kilometer.

Unofficial guesstimates put the population of the town at over 100,000 and of the Valley of Jovel, which is roughly contiguous with the municipio, at 140,000. The 1980 population of the state of Chiapas was officially 2,085,000, and of Tuxtla, the capital, 241,000. Present figures are at least 30 percent higher, all the more so as they are inflated by a substantial Guatemalan immigration of political refugees and undocumented agricultural workers, mostly Indians. Even though all these figures are to be treated as approximations, and probably underestimates by a factor of at least 10 percent, one fact is apparent about the growth of San Cristóbal. It remained fairly slow until 1970 (growing by less than 50 percent between 1950 and 1970), but has been explosive since 1970 (135 percent between 1970 and 1980).

The 1980 census lists 27.7 percent of the population of the state of Chiapas as speakers of indigenous (mostly Mayan) languages. If one estimates the current state population at close to three million, and allows for undercounting (which is generally agreed to be particularly great for Indians, in part because many men are away as migrant workers when the census is taken, and in part because enumeration is spotty in remote rural areas), then a rough figure of one million Indians for Chiapas is probably not far from the truth. In round figures, then, San Cristóbal, the largest urban center for the highlands, is a mostly ladino city of 100,000 surrounded by an overwhelmingly Indian population of one million.

Many other changes accompanied population growth. Road access, and therefore the volume of trade and the mobility of the population, has increased enormously during the past four decades. In 1950, San Cristóbal was accessible only by dirt roads. Now, paved roads connect San Cristóbal with Tuxtla to the west, Comitán, Guatemala, and Tapachula to the east and south; and Villahermosa, Palenque, and the Yucatán Peninsula to the north. All-weather dirt roads now link San Cristóbal with the vast majority of Indian communities, and some, like

Chamula, Zinacantán, Huistán, Oxchuc, and Amatenango, are now served by paved roads and regular bus or *colectivo* service. The number of motor vehicles increased exponentially. In 1950, Indians rarely used wheeled transport. They came to town on foot and carried their goods on their backs, or, if they were well off, by mule. Today, scores of Volkswagen microbuses carry people and produce to and from the central market of San Cristóbal and the Indian communities (fig. 11). For the nearer ones, such as Zinacantán and Chamula, one seldom has to wait more than a half-hour for service.

This transportation revolution has, of course, fostered the development of markets, both in San Cristóbal and in the Indian municipios. In the 1950s, the entire market of San Cristóbal fit into the Plaza de la Merced, three blocks west of the Zócalo. After it was moved to the northern outskirts of town, it exploded in size, and now covers some ten hectares, including two supermarkets, a large, covered hall, scores of restaurant stalls, a sprawling bus and *colectivo* terminal with a couple of hundred daily arrivals and departures, and many hundreds of stalls spilling over into the adjacent streets.

Naturally, this greatly increased contact between town and country also affected ethnic relations. Literacy spread in the rural areas, as did knowledge of Spanish among Indians. (De facto, literacy and knowledge of Spanish are nearly coterminous for Indians, as written use of the Mayan languages remains minimal, despite well-meaning efforts by anthropologists, missionaries, and government agents.) The 1980 census gives literacy figures of 69 percent for San Cristóbal, and in the 20 to 40 percent range for Indian municipios (19 percent in Chamula, 31 percent in Zinacantán, 41 percent in Huistán). Of the Indians, between one-third and two-thirds, depending on the municipios, were classified as bilingual in 1980 (34 percent in Chamula, 52 percent in Zinacantán, 57 percent in Huistán). The corresponding figures for Indian literacy and bilingualism in 1950 were in the 10 to 15 percent range.

Many of these transformations in the rural areas were greatly accelerated by the activist stance of the Instituto Nacional Indígenista (the Mexican equivalent of the U.S. Bureau of Indian Affairs, only much more progressive), which opened a large regional center in San Cristóbal in 1948. Since then, INI has implemented an extensive program of rural development, including the building of access roads, the construction of rural schools and clinics, the training of Indian teachers and development workers (known as *promotores*), the publication of schoolbooks and practical manuals in Indian languages, the encouragement of cooperatives to market homespun textiles, and many other rural development activities. Frequently resented by local ladinos, INI saw as part of its mission the protection of Indians against ladino exploitation. Many of its employees were young, urban professionals coming from central Mexico, and university graduates in anthropology, economics, agronomy, and other fields, imbued with a Marxist ideology and activist orientation. INI thus became a ferment of change in ethnic relations. It supported Indians in becoming more self-confident and assertive, and in emancipating them from control and exploitation by local ladinos. The Indian presence in the San Cristóbal market, for instance, has greatly increased. Whereas previously many products grown by Indians were purchased and resold by ladino traders, now most Indians sell their produce directly to the consumers.

INI's efforts in improving the situation of Indians vis-à-vis local ladinos were supplemented by some private initiatives as well. Some resident foreigners, for instance, also helped organize Indian craft cooperatives and foster the marketing of Indian textiles. Protestant denominations encouraged the use of Indian languages in their successful evangelization drives (which did, however, have profoundly disruptive consequences in many Indian communities). The Catholic Church was transformed by liberation theology, and the local clergy became much more progressive, especially the current archbishop, who is seen by the local elite as a radical figure. Foreign anthropologists (especially from Harvard and the University of Chicago), who had long-standing research projects in the area, also left their mark by hiring many Indians as informants, teaching them to be literate in their own language, and sponsoring mother-tongue literacy programs for both children and adults. Many of these Indian informants became prominent in their respective communities and gained self-respect through association with prestigeful outsiders.

Not only do Indians come to San Cristóbal in greatly increasing number and frequency. Many more Indians, principally Chamulas, now live in town, mostly in peripheral slums. The 1980 census is eloquent in this respect. It listed 34,600 persons over fifteen years of age for the municipio of San Cristóbal (a little over half of the total population of 61,000). Of these adults, it classified 69 percent as literate (76 percent of the males, 58 percent of the females). More surprising, the 1980 census also listed 16,200 inhabitants of San Cristóbal over five as speakers of Indian languages, of whom 67 percent were bilingual in Spanish, and 33 percent monolingual. Allowing for children under 5, at least 20,000 of the town's 61,000 inhabitants (roughly one-third) were Indians! Projecting these figures to today's probable San Cristóbal population of over 100,000, this means that some 35,000 Indians now live in and around San Cristóbal.

Until the 1960s, San Cristóbal was almost exclusively a ladino town. A few Indians lived in town, to be sure, mostly domestic servants in middle- and upper-class ladino households. A few more Indians stayed overnight when they came to market, often with ladino *compadres* who gave them *posada* (lodging) as part of their *compadrazgo* relationship. The jail also housed a couple of hundred Indians, some long-term prisoners guilty of witchcraft-induced murders or assaults, but mostly drunks kept overnight and made to sweep the town clean before being released the next day. In short, Indian residents of town could be counted in the hundreds. San Cristóbal was clearly ladino turf; Indians were overwhelmingly visitors to town.

Clearly, the situation has changed radically. Now, thousands of Indian families, mostly Chamulas, live in town permanently. Most are very poor and live in flimsy housing on the outskirts. They constitute an underemployed subproletariat, and they could be described mostly as squatters living precariously on "invaded" land, without water, electricity, or sanitation services. Yet they have become permanent townspeople. It is equally clear from these statistics that the explosive growth of San Cristóbal in the 1970s was almost entirely due to this massive influx of Indians from neighboring communities, most frequently from the Chamula group. The main impetus for that influx is well known. It is traceable to the success of fundamentalist Protestants in converting Indians, who were then expelled from their communities by village authorities, and lost their houses and land. Left destitute, they became, in effect, internal refugees, and gravitated to San Cristóbal, pushed by desperation rather than attracted by opportunities. Other Protestant converts, however, established new rural communities, some of which have become moderately prosperous. Some of the new urbanites have also improved their economic condition by entering the tourist trade, as we shall see.

Available statistics, then, tell a story of San Cristóbal as a ladino town which grew fairly slowly until 1970, and then exploded, largely as a result of an influx of Indians from nearby communities. What else was happening to the regional economy during that period? First, the agricultural basis of the Indian population became increasingly tenuous. As the population increased, arable and pasture land, already scarce by midcentury, became totally insufficient to sustain life. Today, Chamulas probably grow less than 10 percent of the maize and beans they eat. Zinacantecos, who used to produce and market a substantial surplus of maize, have turned to capital-intensive nonfood crops, principally flowers grown in plastic hothouses. Subsistence peasants became subsubsistence, and had to turn to alternatives for survival.

In increasing numbers and for longer durations, men hire themselves out as agricultural laborers in the large fincas of the lowlands. This is considered highly undesirable work, not only because of low wages but also because climatic conditions expose highland Indians to tropical diseases. To make matters worse, political repression and civil war in neighboring Guatemala, and the even more depressed wages there, bring in a flood of Guatemalans desperate to work for even lower wages than Mexicans (as little as $2 a day, but still twice as much as in Guatemala). The Guatemalan-Mexican border area (which includes Chiapas) experiences, on a smaller scale and at a lower level of economic development, a situation similar to that of the Mexican–U.S. border.

During the oil boom of the 1970s, many Indians went to work as unskilled day laborers in the oilfields, in urban construction, or in public works. But then came the crash of 1982, and the long economic depression which plagued the rest of the decade. Meanwhile, in the Chiapas highlands the economy was expanding somewhat, but it remained almost exclusively a tertiary-sector economy based on transportation, artisanal production, and retail trade. San Cristóbal still lacks modern industry. It does not have a single factory, and its secondary sector is made up of small back-patio workshops producing textiles on pedal looms; furniture and coffin shops employing a carpenter and two or three apprentices; sidewalk cobblers hammering together sandals (huaraches) from leather thongs and old tires; and the like. Except for a few diesel and electrical engines, San Cristóbal's secondary industry still uses basically eighteenth-century technology and social organization.

What, then, explains not only the town's rapid recent growth but its relative prosperity, in the midst of a national depression? The answer is tourism.

THE GROWTH OF TOURISM

When I first came to San Cristóbal in 1959, tourists were a rarity. The town had three small hotels, each with eight to ten rooms, but even they were not primarily oriented to tourist traffic. The best, the Hotel Español, which still exists, was clean and attractive but quite modest. Its restaurant, which charged rather less than a dollar for a five- or six-course lunch, was considered a cornucopia of gastronomic delights by the little team of anthropologists from the Harvard Chiapas Project to which I belonged. The only other "decent" place to eat as a paying guest was Na Bolom, another still extant fixture of the San Cristóbal scene, but it, too, rather stretched the budget of a graduate student (I seem to remember that it charged a steep $1.50 for lunch, but our total two-person budget for three months was $500, including car expenses). It was, at best, a weekly treat. The Santa Clara Hotel, where we briefly stayed before renting a small flat in one of the town's rare three-story buildings, was, except for electricity, an unmodernized sixteenth-century adobe house with a single rudimentary bathroom. Don Joaquín, a political refugee of the Spanish Civil War, who named his store, La Segoviana, after his hometown, was a pioneer of the tourist trade. He was the first one to stock local Indian textiles for sale to outsiders, but, in those days, I suspect his clients were more anthropologists, archaeologists, and other resident gringos than real tourists.

The Bloms, Franz until his death in 1963 and his legendary wife Trudy (fig. 26) who at eighty-eight has become San Cristóbal's grande dame, were also pioneers of tourism. In fact, they could be considered the local inventors of "adventure tourism." Their house, Na Bolom (a Tzotzil pun, meaning both House of the Jaguar and House of Blom), a large, rambling nineteenth-century structure on the eastern edge of town, was (and still is) at once a little private museum, a research library, a meeting place for resident artists and social scientists, and a guest house for the occasional well-heeled gringos seeking the thrill of adventure and the illusion of exploration without any of the risks (fig. 26). Trudy would organize a mule train for them and take them down to the rain forest to visit the ruins of Bonampak and the famed and romanticized Lacandón Indians, *tous frais compris*. Franz Blom said then that he did not want to see the day when Indians would dress in Western clothes, and tourists would dress as Indians. His wish was fulfilled (he died in 1963), but his widow has seen his prophecy come to pass. Chamula women now buy secondhand Western clothes for their children on the market, while counterculture tourists bedecked in Indian textiles bought in a half-dozen different villages share a surreptitious hash joint in La Familia, San Cristóbal's "hippie nest" (to use a local informant's phrase, *un nido de ipis*). The Lacandones whom Trudy helped "put on the map" and romanticize as the purest, most authentic descendants of the Maya, now come to San Cristóbal to peddle their "stone-age" bows and arrows to tourists, and even (as I witnessed) to other Indians who had come to San Cristóbal for a government-sponsored "national encounter of indigenous peoples" (fig. 37). "Leave them in peace," she now pleads with the descendants of the first tourists she took to see the exotic, noble savages. But the genie of tourism which she uncorked will not go back into the bottle.

Most local observers of the tourist scene and long-term participants in it seem to agree that tourism went roughly through three stages. Precise dates cannot be assigned because they gradually merged into one another, and because the different modal types of tourists which characterized each did not so much vanish in the succeeding phases as superimpose themselves on the previous types. During the incipient period, from roughly the late 1950s to the late 1960s, tourists were principally middle-aged, fairly affluent, and adventuresome North Americans who came, mostly as couples or nuclear families, in their own car, camper, or trailer, but who occasionally flew in as well. (In those days, San Cristóbal had a short and perilous landing strip, facing a hillside, where an old 1930s-vintage, three-engined Junker regularly landed. The strip still exists and is occasionally used by helicopters, but it is unsuited for modern planes, and the area surrounding it is too built up for regular landings to be safe.) The few tourists either drove down the recently paved Pan American Highway, and stopped for a day or two in San Cristóbal on their way to Central America, or they came for a couple of weeks to go on a Lacandón jungle trip with Trudy.

In the absence of records, it is difficult to reconstruct the volume of that traffic, but from recollections of my 1959 fieldwork, I would say that the numbers seldom exceeded ten on any given day, often much less. A new car with foreign plates on the Zócalo was a minor sensation and a highly visible one, as the entire population of private cars in town probably did not exceed fifty, and as public bus traffic was virtually nonexistent. One seldom saw more than five or six cars together on the Zócalo. Traffic lights were not even dreamed of, and the movements of any vehicle were always followed with some interest, as they coincided with the whereabouts of important people. Only VIPs could afford cars, and the latter were few enough that they could be associated with their owners. (Even my battered black Volkswagen beetle was a status symbol and a calling card.)

In absolute numbers, this type of tourism continues to increase. Relatively, however, it is now greatly eclipsed by the later types. The second phase of San Cristóbal tourism began in the late 1960s and dominated the next fifteen years or so, until the early 1980s. Local observers usually describe it as *turismo pobre* ("poor tourism") or *turismo de mochila* ("backpack tourism"), and tend to denigrate it as not very profitable, yet there is no question that it was that new type of tourist who spread the fame of San Cristóbal around the world, and became a pathbreaker for the third wave (fig. 32). Backpack tourists started "discovering" San Cristóbal as a cheap and quaint "must" on the Central American "hippie trail" early in the development of this type of "alternative" tourism. In terms of national origin, Europeans outnumbered North Americans by three or four to one, with a strong French, German, Italian, Swiss, Dutch, and Scandinavian representation. The Japanese were latecomers to the backpack crowd. Backpackers continued to grow during that period, starting with scores and ending with hundreds a day, peaking in the summer months, but not limited to them.

Backpack tourists were mostly young, childless adults ranging in age from eighteen to thirty-five, traveling either alone or in twos (either couples or friends), but also forming temporary aggregations of up to a half-dozen through chance encounters on the road, sharing lodgings to reduce expenses. Most were certainly not "hippies," but simply young, educated people (students, teachers, professionals) traveling mostly by public bus or train, and wanting to spend much time (often several months) on the road, experiencing foreign countries at some depth, making an effort to learn the language, and stretching their money so that the pleasant, exciting learning experience would last. For most, it was their first extended stay out of their own cultures, and thus all the more exciting. They chose Mexico because to them it was exotic, colorful, safe, warm, and cheap, and they loved San Cristóbal because it was even better than the rest of Mexico in terms of their criteria of attractiveness. So they spread the word among their friends. (For accounts of backpack tourism elsewhere, see Cohen 1979c, 1982a; Riley 1988; and Weiler and Hall 1992.)

After a few years, guidebooks (such as the French *Guide du Routard*, the Australian *Lonely Planet*, and the German *Anders Reisen*) began to cater to this type of tourism, but the backpack tourist tends to be individualistic, only moderately sociable, contemptuous of "typical" tourists, anticonsumerist, budget conscious, and highly adaptable to local diet and conditions of transport and housing. He buys little because he has to carry what he buys (although he may periodically ship a package of purchases home from the local post office). He tries to make sure that he does not pay more for food, handicrafts, or services than the going rate for locals, and resents it as evidence of his incompetence if he is cheated. Above all, he wants to be called a traveler, not a tourist. He often recognizes the irony of his presence spoiling his quest for the exotic, and thus he tries to be an unobtrusive and undemanding tourist. Basically, he asks his hosts simply to be themselves.

As backpack tourists began to proliferate in San Cristóbal, so did the establishments catering to their demands. The 1970s saw an explosion in the number of small, modest, locally owned one- and two-star hotels, posadas, and eateries, either in a clean, unpretentious, starkly utilitarian "Mexican modern" style or in simple, attractive adaptations or imitations of colonial architecture. Backpack tourists typically demanded little more than safety and cleanliness, and they got them. They were satisfied to sleep several to a room, to share baths and toilets, and to buy their food from street vendors, but they also appreciated a good pizza or hamburger, or a cheap, tasty *comida corrida* (luncheon special) in a restaurant catering mostly to locals. They detested the "touristy" and hated being treated as tourists.

Relations with locals seem to have remained good, and San Cristóbal largely escaped the drug scene (except for a little marijuana smoking, and even that was quite furtive), because of Mexico's well-deserved reputation for incarcerating foreign junkies in unpleasant jails. Locals seem to have only one major complaint about backpack tourists: they do not spend as much money as locals would like. Indeed, most of them spend less than Mexican tourists of the same social class or income level. Mexicans frequently mistake a frugal travel style for poverty, hence the misnomer *turismo pobre* applied to the backpack tourist. The young art student from Geneva, for example, wearing artfully torn and discolored jeans and eating corn-on-the-cob in the market like a common Indian may look poor to a local who does not know that she can afford to take a six-month vacation slumming through Latin America because her parents offered her the trip as a graduation present.

What problems locals had about backpack tourists not spending enough were solved by the third wave, beginning in the early 1980s: the conducted, package tours, which now descend like manna on San Cristóbal hotels at the rate of half a dozen busloads or so per day. Composed mostly of batches of twenty-five to forty middle-aged or "young elderly" Europeans from the same country or even city who bought a one- to three-week, all-inclusive package tour of Mexico (or Mexico and Guatemala), these group tourists usually just stay in San Cristóbal overnight (fig. 33). They seem more affluent because they wear more expensive clothes and jewelry, carry matched designer luggage, and spend more time and money in curio shops than the backpack tourists. It is true that they spend between $100 and $200 a day per person (not including airfare), compared to the typical budget of $10 to $25 a day of the backpacker. However, most of their money does not stay in San Cristóbal, and their stay is much shorter.

Nonetheless, most local entrepreneurs in the tourist industry love the third wave and see it as an unending rainbow to future affluence. In particular, the recent *National Geographic* article, "La Ruta Maya" (Garrett and Garrett 1989), lights up dollar signs in the eyes of San Cristóbal hoteliers and restaurateurs, all the more so as San Cristóbal clearly appears as a stopover on the four-country, 2,500 kilometer circuit. The glossy photography and the authors' alluring vision of "a cable way or monorail through environmentally sensitive areas" and "quality bus service with a Eurail-type pass" (Garrett and Garrett 1989:436) is enough to make the three-star hotelier see himself as a Mexican Donald Trump. Little does he realize that the third wave is likely to chase away the second wave, and that nothing is more fickle than the fashionableness of package-tour destinations: yesterday Cuzco, today Katmandu, tomorrow Timbuktu (Butler and Waldbrook 1991; Plog 1974). For now, at any rate, the prospects for San Cristóbal look good. The town even became the feature article of the travel section of the *New York Times* under the title "Rockets of San Cristóbal: A Colonial City in the Highlands of Southern Mexico Celebrates Year Round" (Porter 1990:14). The nonstop fiesta in the land of eternal spring: what more can the tourist's heart desire?

THE TOURIST IMPACT

Let us conclude this chapter by attempting to assess the magnitude of the tourist impact on San Cristóbal today, in terms of both employment and income. As we shall see from conservative estimates reconstructed from piecemeal data in Chapter 4, tourism brings a minimum of $5 million annually into San Cristóbal's economy. Furthermore, nearly all of that money stays in the local economy because it goes to goods and services owned and controlled by local ladinos and Indians. Naturally, not all of that is profit, nor are the benefits of tourism equally distributed. Perhaps twenty or thirty of the leading ladino hotel, restaurant, and shop owners skim off the lion's share of the profits, and derive a solid income from tourism which guarantees them a place in the town's economic elite. Indeed, many of them already belonged to the town's elite before the advent of mass tourism. To them, tourism merely offered a broadened scope for entrepreneurship. To this entrepreneurial elite, however, must be added another 200 or so smaller ladino businesses (small restaurants, shops, workshops, posadas, and so on) which secure for their owners a place in the town's petite bourgeoisie.

Further down the class hierarchy, one must include wage earners whose jobs depend directly on the tourist trade. The leading half-dozen hotels employ between 35 and 50 people each; the dozen medium-scale ones, between 8 and 15; small posadas, 3 or 4, for a total of 400 to 500 employees in the hotel branch. Restaurants average 5 to 8 employees for the 20-odd larger ones, 2 or 3 for some 50 smaller ones, in total some 250 to 300 jobs. Some 300 to 400 sales or clerical jobs should be added for the shops, travel agencies, and other services dealing principally with tourists. These estimates add up to roughly 1,000 service, clerical, and sales jobs held overwhelmingly by local ladinos. This figure must be multiplied by at least five to include the dependents of these wage earners who live directly from the tourist industry. These estimates are very close to the national ones. The Secretary of Tourism, Pedro Joaquín Coldwell, estimates that each hotel room adds 1.5 direct jobs and 2.5 indirect ones to the labor force (Suárez 1990). San Cristóbal has some 440 hotel rooms.

At the bottom of the tourism trade is the "street economy" of peripatetic entrepreneurs: hawkers, shoeshiners, beggars, and so on. Composed overwhelmingly of Chamula Indians, most of whom now live in San Cristóbal, that street economy employs at least 250 to 300 people, and this figure must be multiplied by at least six to include their dependents. Finally, at the grass roots, in the Indian villages of San Cristóbal's hinterland, we find thousands of women who produce textiles and pottery which end up in the San Cristóbal tourist market, even though most of these women sell their work to middlemen rather than directly to tourists.

At a minimum, 1,500 townspeople are either owners or employees of businesses selling goods or services primarily to tourists in San Cristóbal itself. A confirmation of this estimate is provided by the Hiernaux and Rodríguez (1990) study, which put 1988 direct employment in tourism in the three Chiapas cities of San Cristóbal, Tuxtla, and Tapachula at 7,238. While Tuxtla and Tapachula are less "touristy" than San Cristóbal, they are much bigger. Of the people living from tourism, some three-fourths are ladinos, and one-fourth Indians, most Chamulas. Applying the multiplier of five to include dependents, some 7,000 to 8,000 townspeople live *directly* from tourism—that is, some 6 to 8 percent of the town's population of over 100,000. The *indirect* impact of tourism on other businesses, crafts, and the like, which in turn build and supply the hotels, restaurants, shops, and so on, affects at least twice or three times as many people. Hiernaux and Rodríguez (1990:10) give a multiplier of 2.81 indirect tourist jobs for every direct job, for Mexico in 1980. At a minimum, 25 percent of the town's population would be much worse off if it were not for tourism. Without doubt, tourism has become San Cristóbal's main industry.

4 TOURISM IN SAN CRISTÓBAL

Despite its 100,000 inhabitants and its rapidly developing urbanity and sophistication, San Cristóbal still looks and feels like a small town. That, of course, is what makes it charming and attractive to tourists. This is no accident. San Cristóbal had the good fortune of remaining a backwater until the 1960s, and owes much of its development to being a tourist attraction. The municipal authorities and the local elite recognized a good thing early enough to impose strict building codes and minimize the construction of reinforced concrete, multistoried structures which now dominate the center of most Mexican cities.

A vision of what the center of San Cristóbal might have become without draconian restrictions is provided by the chaotic ugliness along the Pan-American Highway, on the southern periphery of town. An unsightly, anarchic mixture of large, multistoried public buildings in "Mexican modern," gas stations, supermarkets, Tex-Mex hotels in fake hacienda style, bus depots, grimy repair shops, pretentious villas, and squatters' shacks, the highway strip looks like a Third World version of its North American counterparts. This is not what tourists come to see.

THE LOCAL ECOLOGY OF TOURISM

The heart of town—the six to eight blocks extending in all directions from the Zócalo—has preserved its traditional colonial architecture (figs. 1, 2, 4). The tallest buildings, by far, are the dozen or so baroque churches built in the sixteenth to eighteenth centuries, which include the cathedral, the parish churches, and the former convent churches (fig. 4). Even the churches were sufficiently modest and provincial in colonial days not to be able to afford high spires. The Torre del Carmen (fig. 12), a local landmark, belies its name and barely looks over the sea of tiled roofs by a few meters. Except for a jarring commercial building near the Zócalo which sports a miniature Eiffel tower on its fourth-story roof, houses rarely exceed two stories. The town presents a homogeneous picture of one- or two-storied adobe houses, usually whitewashed, with red, Spanish-tiled, overhanging roofs.

Most streets intersect at right angles, in the classical (but somewhat irregular) Spanish grid pattern, with two principal arterials radiating out of each side of the Zócalo (see Map 2, p. 30). Even the principal streets are only seven or eight meters wide. A narrow sidewalk no more than a meter wide on each side leaves barely enough room for two cars to pass one another. Luckily, most streets are one-way, but still, large buses find it difficult to negotiate right turns, and have to plan their itineraries to avoid getting stuck at particularly narrow corners. Clearly, San Cristóbal was not built with the motorcar in mind. Indeed, the town is both small and bustling enough that driving a car in town is more inconvenient than useful, although parking is still no problem. Only the Zócalo and two other intersections sport traffic lights. Rules governing the right-of-way are only spottily observed, but rough pavement, narrow streets, parked vehicles, and jaywalking pedestrians luckily combine to keep velocity, and thus accidents, down.

Most churches are built on a little plaza, usually one city block in size, where trees provide shade and greenery, and stone or wrought-iron benches an inviting resting place or outdoor parlor. Some of these small parks are quiet and devoid of commercial activity, but two are very busy during most of the day, especially between 9 a.m. and 2 p.m.

The Zócalo is the civic heart of town (see figs. 7, 8, 19). On its north side is the stately cathedral; the west side is occupied by the long Grecian facade of the town hall (fig. 13), which houses most government offices including the police headquarters, tourist office, civil registry, and tax office; two of the best hotels, a bank, and a couple of shops share the southern side; and a long arcade filled with street vendors and flanked by a dozen businesses form the east side (fig. 19). The Zócalo park, shaded by palm trees, has star-patterned footpaths converging on a wrought-iron band kiosk converted into a café. Along the footpaths, wrought-iron benches invite passersby to stop, and a score or so of strategically posted shoeshiners wait in ambush (fig. 8). From the late morning to the early evening hours, most benches are occupied by ladino townsmen, visiting Indians and tourists alike, though the three groups seldom mix and interact on the Zócalo.

In the early evening hours, especially on weekends, the Zócalo becomes the favorite meeting ground of the unmarried, as groups of young ladino men and women walk past, ogling each other. Not infrequently, a music or dance event livens a weekend evening, as might an evening service in the cathedral or the end of the picture show at the nearby cinema. Popcorn, hot dog, and beverage carts and stands lit by kerosene lanterns, and the floodlit facade of the cathedral and town hall, make a colorful scene. A few tourists also mill around in the evening crowd, but the Zócalo at night is mostly ladino turf.

The second busy plaza is the large one linking the churches of Santo Domingo and La Caridad (see Map 2). Beautifully shaded by secular trees, it constitutes the most attractive ensemble of colonial architecture in San Cristóbal (fig. 4). Until a decade or so ago, it was almost totally devoid of commercial activity and was bathed in an atmosphere of cloistered quietude. The growing tourist traffic transformed it into a hub of activity. The plaza has been taken over by between one and two hundred Chamula women (and an even greater number of their young children), who spread their wares for sale to tourists. Thus it has become the principal meeting ground of tourists and tourees (figs. 10, 20, 21). It is also conveniently on Avenida Utrilla (fig. 35), the main street linking the Zócalo and the large produce market on the northern edge of town.

By far the busiest place in San Cristóbal, especially from 8 a.m. to 4 p.m., is the sprawling produce market (figs. 11, 39). It attracts thousands of Indian vendors and customers from neighboring villages every day, and almost equal numbers of town ladinos. If one includes the adjacent streets and bus terminals into which the market has expanded in recent years, it now covers about eight to ten hectares, and is even beginning to spill over across the Rio Amarillo (an open sewer that perhaps should be renamed Rio Basurero). The core of the produce market is made up of three large recent buildings: a hall filled with scores of meat, fruit, vegetable, and other stalls, and two supermarkets. Around these large buildings are hundreds of outdoor stalls, a row of little restaurants, many stores and warehouses in the adjacent streets, a second-class bus station, and a large open area with several rows of stands for microbuses (fig. 11).

Every available square meter of open space in that labyrinth of stores and stalls is further occupied by hundreds of Indian women who display their produce on the ground in front of them, leaving passageways just wide enough for dollies and wheeled garbage cans. A few of the more adventuresome tourists make it to the big market, but they seldom stay more than ten or fifteen minutes and their numbers seldom exceed twenty or thirty at any given time, among several thousand locals, both ladinos and Indians. Most tourists find the produce market too odorous, crowded, unsanitary, and noisy for their taste. Moreover, they fear the few cruising pickpockets who give the place a bad name.

TOURIST FACILITIES, SIGHTS, AND DISTRIBUTION

The city of San Cristóbal stretches over some seven or eight square kilometers, but at least 95 percent of the tourist traffic concentrates in a narrow north-south corridor linking the produce market to the Pan-American Highway (see Map 2). The two points are connected by a street named Utrilla until it touches the northeastern corner of the Zócalo, and Insurgentes between the Zócalo and the first-class bus station of the Cristóbal Colón line on the highway. At least two-thirds of all commercial establishments and "points of interest" visited by tourists are to be found within two blocks east or west of that axis. A circle 500 meters in radius with the Zócalo at its center encompasses nearly all of tourist San Cristóbal, except for the produce market, Na Bolom, the bus stations, the two campgrounds, and a handful of hotels which are just beyond that range.

Insurgentes-Utrilla is clearly the main tourist "drag," plus a three-block section of Calle Real de Guadalupe that intersects it from the east at the Zócalo. A dozen of the town's twenty-one two- and three-star hotels, and a similar proportion of the twenty or so better restaurants frequented by tourists, are either on it or within 200 meters of it on side streets. This is even truer of the seventy-five or so shops selling primarily *artesanías* (handicrafts) to tourists. Some 90 percent are to be found on these streets, three clusters of them in *galerías* (with a fourth one under construction). The Chamula open-air craft market around the Santo Domingo and Caridad churches is on the west side of Utrilla, halfway between the Zócalo and the produce market. In short, tourists stepping off a first-class bus and walking 1,500 meters to the north run an uninterrupted gauntlet of hotels, posadas (smaller pensions), restaurants, cafés, boutiques, bookstores, gift shops, and textile cooperatives designed to get them to stop and part with some of their money. They would also, in their twenty-minute walk, have passed within sight of nearly all they are likely to see of San Cristóbal in an average stay of one or two days.

Due to this high concentration of tourist facilities and attractions, the tourist presence in San Cristóbal can be perceived in very paradoxical ways. Walking up and down three or four streets within two or three blocks of the Zócalo, one gains the impression that the town is "crawling" with tourists, even though tourists probably seldom exceed one percent of the population on any given day. On average, some 400 arrive each day and stay 1.6 days, according to tourist office statistics for the last three years. Thus somewhere around 600 to 650 tourists are in town on an average day, with perhaps half as many during the low months and close to a thousand during the peak summer season. The town's

440 hotel rooms have occupancy rates of slightly above 50 percent most of the year, but most of these rooms are doubles, and these statistics (from the Oficina de Turismo) do not include some of the modest posadas. It is thus possible for one percent or less of the population to be quite visible by concentrating in a central location and consuming the bulk of the town's luxury services. Indeed, many tourists complain of how touristy the town is becoming, a good indication that their stated aversion to the presence of other tourists does not prevent them from being attracted by the same limited range of sites.

The other side of the paradox is that one need only walk to one of the many quiet residential side streets, even within three or four blocks of the Zócalo, to avoid seeing any tourists for hours. Tourists are both easy to find and easy to avoid. Depending on where one is, by chance or by design, the town can seem either full of tourists or almost empty of them. This choice has, I believe, important implications for tourist-touree relations: one is less likely to resent the presence of someone one has the option of avoiding.

HOTELS

One of the great charms of San Cristóbal for the kind of tourist it attracts is that it lacks any of the standard five-star chain hotels. That situation might change, since Club Méditerranée owns a large piece of land and is persistently rumored to plan the construction of a large hotel. Many local ladinos associated with the tourist trade think luxury hotels would greatly boost the tourist manna descending on San Cristóbal, but my impression is that the type of ethnic tourist attracted by San Cristóbal would stop coming, and, conversely, that San Cristóbal has little to offer to the sun-sand-and-sea, $100-a-day tourist in search of an expensive playground.

Local response to tourist demand for lodging has, in my view, been remarkably appropriate and successful. In 1988, San Cristóbal had twenty-one hotels, mostly in the three- and two-star categories (though one recently received its fourth star and another is in the process of applying for it). All were Mexican owned, and nearly all were owned by local San Cristóbal people or their spouses, or by proprietors from neighboring Chiapas towns. Most of the owners were directly involved in the management of their property, though the larger hotels typically had managers as well. In addition to this score of hotels, another score of more modest establishments called posadas (pensions) or casas de huéspedes (guesthouses) offer frugal backpack tourists more Spartan, but still clean and safe, accommodations.

In the two- and three-star hotels, the tourist can expect, for prices ranging from $10 to $25 for a double room, a clean, comfortable, often spacious room with a private bath, hot water, and, in the three-star category, television and telephone in each room. A dozen of these establishments (including several of the more modest ones) are located in modernized colonial mansions with beam-ceiling rooms, attractive patios with fountains and luxuriant vegetation, and an exotic ambiance that enchants ethnic tourists (figs. 27, 28, 29). A half-dozen or so are neocolonial attempts to recreate an old atmosphere, but the small, utilitarian rooms and the long rectilinear corridors invariably spoil the effect. The remaining hotels and posadas are clean but unpretentious cement block buildings in "Mexican modern." The simpler and cheaper ones have shared baths, but the rooms and the bathrooms are still clean and adequate, if bare and graceless.

At the upper end of the scale, hotel lobbies, corridors, dining rooms, and guest rooms are decorated with posters and photographs of local Indians, of archaeological sites (especially of Palenque, a Chiapas Maya ruin and a frequent next stop for passing tourists), and of San Cristóbal churches; with local artifacts (especially Indian textiles, pottery, and Lacandón bows and arrows); with tourist maps of Mexico and Chiapas; and, in a few cases, with wall frescoes having contemporary or archaeological Maya motifs (figs. 40, 41). Similar decorations adorn the better restaurants and the tourist office (figs. 30, 31). Whether in the archaeological past or the ethnographic present, Maya themes feature prominently in attempts by tourist establishments to appeal to their clientele. Indeed, a number of hotels, restaurants, shops, and travel agencies use Maya names such as Jovel ("grass" in Tzotzil, the name of the valley of San Cristóbal), Tuluc ("wild turkey"), Bonampak (a Maya ruin), Pakal (the name of the young king buried in the pyramid of Palenque), and Na Bolom (House of the Jaguar), to name but a few.

In addition to the hotels, two expatriates have turned their large homes into expensive accommodations for well-heeled paying guests who reserve in advance, often come by plane to Tuxtla, stay a week or longer, and want to avoid the promiscuity of hotels (fig. 26). Both of these guesthouses are elegantly furnished with antiques and crafts, and charge considerably more than the best hotels.

Only seven hotels could be described as medium size, with thirty or more rooms (sixty or more beds). The largest, and, according to some, the best, named after San Cristóbal's conquistador, Diego de Mazariegos (figs. 22, 28, 33), has seventy-seven rooms, and it consists of two adjacent but completely separate colonial mansions, each of which is about the same size as other larger hotels. Most of the other hotels have between fifteen and twenty-five rooms, and the posadas between six and ten rooms. Several hotels are building extensions, despite an average occupancy rate of barely over half. All but a handful of hotels and posadas opened after 1970, over half in the last decade, and the booming supply anticipates an ever-growing demand.

RESTAURANTS

The restaurant scene covers roughly the same qualitative range as the hotels and posadas, from the small market stalls and holes-in-the-wall charging about $1.50 for a *comida corrida* (luncheon special) to the elegant restaurants where a meal can cost up to $10 or $12 with wine. Eighteen of the hotels have dining rooms with complete meal service, but most of the best restaurants are unconnected to hotels. The vast majority of eating places, like the hotels, are owned by local ladinos, but a half-dozen are owned and operated by resident expatriates (who are often married to Mexicans).

Altogether, there are some seventy restaurants and cafés in town, including the eighteen hotel dining rooms, but not counting the thirty-odd simple eateries in the produce market. Of these establishments, no more than twenty to thirty are regularly frequented by tourists. In most of the best ten or twelve restaurants, the clientele is about equally divided between tourists and local ladinos, but there are five or six eating places that cater almost exclusively to tourists and resident gringos, and serve mostly non-Mexican foods (such as yogurt shakes, whole-grain bread, quiche, and pizzas). Most of them are also run by non-Mexicans and serve as hangouts for resident expatriates (mostly British and American). There is also a counterculture hangout, La Familia, better known for its evening music and company than for the quality of its food.

At the lower end of the scale, small hole-in-the-wall eateries are undecorated, and serve simple Mexican food. A single smallish room contains a cooking counter, four to six small tables, and often a toilet behind a wooden partition in the corner. An occasional backpack tourist may eat there, but most of the clientele consists of local ladinos. The market eating stalls are run by ladinos but patronized principally by Indians, though also by a rare adventuresome backpack tourist. There are also a few fast-food, stand-up restaurants selling mostly hamburgers and ice cream, and these tend to cater mostly to the younger set of both local ladinos and tourists. Inexpensive food can also be bought from street vendors, especially corn-on-the-cob, *atole* (a hot, thick, maize drink), *palomitas* (popcorn), a great variety of pastries and candies, hot dogs, and tacos. Quite a few of the younger backpack tourists buy from street vendors, and go to the market to purchase fresh and baked goods.

By contrast, the upscale restaurants tend to be larger (though they rarely have more than fifteen to twenty tables) and to be more decorated, in much the same way as the better hotels, with Indian artifacts, posters, and photographs. The food is generally more Europeanized (mostly in the French or Italian direction), although it also includes some Mexican specialties, and the menu is sometimes multilingual (Spanish, English, and French mostly). One or more of the waiters will often know a smattering of French, English, or even German. Some of the restaurants are decorated around a theme (El Teatro, El Unicornio, El Oasis). At least a dozen are located in restored colonial houses; some have attractive patios; three boast good views of town. Finally, there is some specialization in types of food. La Langosta serves seafood (not an obvious choice at 2,100 meters above sea level); La Parilla specializes in grilled steaks; Super Pollo dishes out fried chicken, and so on. The Shanghai and the Jardín Yin-Yang share the clientele for Chinese food (or some approximation thereto). (The Jardín Yin-Yang provides a vaguely Chinese-sounding music produced on an African thumb-piano, Caribbean drums, and sundry bells by a black San Franciscan, and the authenticity of its food matches that of the music, though both are quite acceptable in their own right.)

One restaurant, El Fogón de Jovel, lays on the local color most thickly and is rewarded with an almost exclusively tourist clientele. It serves its food in a covered patio which contains a replica of an Indian house altar. A ladina dressed as an Indian can be seen patting and baking tortillas on a charcoal adobe oven. A two-man marimba band plays Chiapas music, and the two ladino waiters are dressed, one as a Chamula and the other as a Zinacanteco.

TOURIST SHOPS, HAWKERS, AND BEGGARS

Competition for the tourist "curio" dollar is stiffest of all, for curios and crafts are discretionary expenditures par excellence. Therefore, location is even more at a premium than for hotels and restaurants. Many tourists will gladly walk one or two extra blocks for a recommended hotel or restaurant. Few actively seek out curio shops. They "stumble into them," and most of their purchases are on impulse, not planned in advance. There are exceptions, of course, as when one looks for a particular item (such as a machete promised to a grandson, or a designer dress from a particular boutique recommended by another traveler), or when one is on a buying as well as a pleasure trip, financing one's travels through the resale of native crafts. Much more common, especially for the backpack tourist, is the predicament of having to restrain one's impulse to buy local crafts in order to keep traveling light. Fragile, ponderous crafts like pottery meet particularly strong sales resistance, while weaving is in a privileged position. Textiles are relatively light and unbreakable, and many of them can be worn.

In San Cristóbal, sales to tourists consist overwhelmingly of handmade textiles, woven, embroidered, or braided by Indian women, either from Mexico or from neighboring Guatemala (figs. 17, 20, 21, 22, 23, 44). In second and third positions come probably leather goods (belts, hats, coats, sandals, and so on) and amber jewelry, both trades being almost exclusively ladino controlled (figs. 24, 36). Pottery, mostly from

Amatenango, is seen everywhere in San Cristóbal, and used by locals as cheap patio planters and decorations, but little of it is sold to tourists for reasons already mentioned, and also because local pottery is much less striking than the glazed, multicolored ceramic found in central Mexico or the black pottery of Oaxaca.

Selling crafts to tourists is a vast, complicated endeavor in San Cristóbal, but one which is spatially highly concentrated. Most of it is confined to an L-shaped area which begins at the northern end of the Santo Domingo market, follows the five blocks of Utrilla Avenue south to the northeastern corner of the Zócalo, and then turns eastward along four blocks of Calle Real de Guadalupe. On this itinerary are found three Indian textile cooperatives (fig. 23), the big Chamula market between the two churches (figs. 10, 20, 21, 44), three galleries, each with a cluster of shops, and a long chain of stores dedicated either entirely or at least partly to the tourist trade (figs. 19, 35). Bookstores and office supply businesses, for instance, stock guidebooks, maps, postcards, and publications about the town, local Indians, or nearby ruins. Pharmacies are well stocked in antidiarrhea remedies and so on. La Segoviana, Don Joaquín's large store, is the ancestor of all curio shops, and is located, appropriately enough, in the elbow of the L, at the corner of Utrilla and Guadalupe, next to a fancy new gallery, and very near an even fancier one in the making. A few more upscale shops, however, notably La Galería (fig. 27), and three fashion boutiques are located outside the L, though no more than a couple of blocks away.

Even though it is encompassed in such a small space, the craft market is extremely complex and internally differentiated, involving thousands of Indian women weavers, hundreds of ladino middlemen, a score or so of resident expatriates, and even, on the fringe of it, some tourists who sell their own crafts to other tourists. There is also a hierarchy of prices, tastes, and investments ranging from highly capitalized, well-stocked businesses in large, stylish stores, to Chamula street vendors carrying their entire stock of bracelets and belts in a little bag.

At the top of the market are businesses catering exclusively to the more affluent and discriminating tourist and to the Mexican elite. La Galería, next to a restaurant by the same name, is in a lavishly restored colonial house half a block from the Zócalo, and sells carefully chosen pottery, blankets, rugs, *huipiles* (blouses), masks, papier-mâché dolls, and the like from other Mexican states rather than local crafts. Another store on the Zócalo sells Oneida silverware from the United States and porcelain from the People's Republic of China, and seems to cater mostly to Mexican tourists and the local elite. A third establishment in one of the galleries off Guadalupe Street has a small stock of real and fake antiques as well as high quality Guatemalan textiles. Some more specialized shops sell jewelry, art books, stained glass lampshades, and so on. A young Frenchman, for instance, markets the artistic silver jewelry made by his Mexican father-in-law. Indeed, at the upper end of the scale, at least half a dozen of the merchants are foreigners: a couple of Frenchmen, a Canadian, and a German, among others.

In a special category are four women (two Mexicans, one Canadian, and one American) who design and make clothes inspired by local traditions, incorporate local Indian weavings in their designs, and even produce homespun fabrics on large pedal looms. Each heads a local cottage industry, and between them they employ several hundred Mexican and Guatemalan Indian women who weave for them and are paid on a piecework basis. Three of them have local outlets in San Cristóbal, but all sell to other stores in Mexico and abroad. The Canadian, in fact, sends nearly her entire production to her mother, who has a hotel in Victoria, B.C., and the American produces an elegant catalogue with fabric samples for sale to various U.S. outlets. The two Mexicans cater to a somewhat less exclusive clientele, have lower prices, and export only to other tourist centers in Mexico, like Cancún, Oaxaca, and Mexico City.

Also in a special category are several Indian-run and operated weavers' cooperatives selling authentic, high quality weavings from all the Indian communities of Chiapas. The oldest, largest, and best known, Na Jolóbil ("House of Weaving" in Tzotzil; see fig. 23), was organized by an American who also assembled a large textile collection now exhibited in the INAH museum and who published several art books on the region (Morris 1984, 1987). It is located in the cloister of the ex-convent of Santo Domingo, in a prime tourist location, and does a thriving business. Another cooperative was organized by INI, a third by a German, and a fourth by the Archdiocese, but they seem less successful, in part because they are less well located. Coop prices are higher than in other stores, but their stock is of uniformly high quality and authenticity. That is, they sell articles of clothing (*huipiles, rebozos,* ponchos, hats, and so on) of the same design, style, and quality as those worn by Indians themselves, plus a few tourist-modified little items (mostly purses and bags) made from small pieces of intricate weaving using traditional designs. These cooperatives sell the work of hundreds of weavers in scores of Indian communities of the region, such as Zinacantán, Chamula, San Andrés, Amatenango, Chenalho, Magdalenas, Tenejapa, Carranza, and others.

The next category of shops, numbering around one hundred, might be described as the "general tourist store," carrying unspecialized and largely interchangeable wares that include principally Mexican and Guatemalan textiles, mostly low quality, made-for-tourists items such as bags, purses, belts, dresses, and so on, but also a few authentic *huipiles* (often used) similar to those sold in the cooperatives (figs. 35, 36). These stores also sell a wide assortment of leather goods, hats, machetes, Lacandón bows and arrows, postcards, pottery, and a few items of inexpensive silver or amber jewelry. Most wares come from Chiapas or from Guatemala (where prices are lower than in Mexico), but some of the larger of these shops, such as La Segoviana, also import a few items (like Charro hats, hammocks, silver jewelry, and pottery) from other Mexican states. The Guatemalan products are imported in bales or suitcases by Guatemalan traveling salesmen who cross the border by bus and sell, often on credit, to ladino store owners or to Chamula street vendors. Except for the cooperatives and the handful of expatriate merchants, virtually all the shops are owned and operated by local ladinos.

Aside from the stores, a large number of itinerant traders sell on the streets and pack up their wares at night. Within that group, too, there is a hierarchy. At the top is a leather craftsman who parks his microbus on either Utrilla or Guadalupe Street (fig. 24), and uses his vehicle as a salesroom. A group of itinerant ladino brothers monopolize the hammock market in San Cristóbal, and also cover Palenque. Some nonlocal Mexican or foreign craftsmen-cum-tourists sell costume jewelry to other tourists. For example, a Brazilian finances his travels by selling semiprecious stones.

The bottom rung of the tourist trade is occupied by Indian street vendors, who are overwhelmingly (at least 95 percent) Chamula women and girls, numbering perhaps 300 to 400. Some come in daily from San Juan Chamula, but most are Protestants who have been expelled from their community and have sought refuge in San Cristóbal. That class of Indian vendors is itself internally stratified between those who are truly ambulatory, accost tourists on the streets (figs. 25, 37), in the market, in the restaurants, and so on, and sell their own merchandise (almost exclusively braided belts, headbands, and armbands) and a better established and successful group who display a wider range of items (mostly not of their own making, and much imported from Guatemala) on plastic sheets at fixed locations, either in the Santo Domingo market or in some hotels and restaurants (figs. 20, 21, 22).

The latter, better-established group are generally recognized by ladinos as an asset to the town because their very presence is a tourist attraction, and because their style of sale is nonaggressive and outwardly noncompetitive. They let customers approach them and look at leisure, with little open solicitation or interference from neighboring sellers. This "laid-back" style is also liked by tourists. Many of these sellers are well enough established that their wares form one or two large bales, which are repacked every evening, transported on dollies (fig. 20), and stored home overnight.

The ambulatory vendors, on the other hand, are generally considered a nuisance by town ladinos, by tourists, and by their Indian competition. They accost tourists repeatedly and persistently, blocking their passage on a narrow sidewalk, pestering them during meals, interrupting conversations, interfering with picture taking, and so on. Their trading is technically illegal, but attempts by the municipal authorities to control them have been desultory, and they are irrepressibly ubiquitous. Driven by grinding poverty, they are irresistibly attracted by the daily presence of hundreds of affluent potential customers. They make many sales because their wares are cheap (from 5 or 6 cents for a bracelet to $1.10 for a belt), attractive, and lightweight, but their margin of profit is very low. A woman and her daughters are lucky to net one or two dollars a day over the cost of raw materials, making their labor worth only a few cents an hour. The sedentary market sellers probably average five or six times as much, but with wide daily fluctuations. They sell many more items in the $3 to $10 range, though with less frequency.

A brief mention should also be made of two other groups of street entrepreneurs: shoeshiners and beggars. Shoeshiners are themselves stratified in a two-class system. Adult ladino men, some fifteen of them, post themselves strategically at fixed locations on the Zócalo. They shine shoes for both locals and tourists, provide their customers with a chair, and give a better class of service (fig. 8). They charge locals 1,000 pesos (35 cents), but generally ask tourists for 2,000 pesos. Besides this "official" group of adult, sedentary shoeshiners, some ten or twelve ladino boys around ten to fourteen years of age roam the Santo Domingo market with little wooden boxes, actively solicit business, and cater almost exclusively to tourists. Their work is of lower quality because their equipment is much more limited, and they work for as little as 500 pesos, but they ask for as much as 4,000 pesos, and usually hold out for a 1,000 peso minimum.

Finally, beggars constitute an interesting group of street entrepreneurs, a few of whom derive a substantial income from tourists. Both Indians and ladinos beg, but the ladino beggars tend to be more professional. Most of the female beggars are Chamula women, usually with a baby and one or two young children, who accost primarily tourists. They usually resort to a pity-inspiring whining strategy, but one (without children) specializes in stretching her arm through open car windows at traffic light stops, peremptorily demanding 500 pesos. An elderly Indian man uses the technique of gently tugging one's sleeve to attract attention and stretching an open palm with a 50 peso coin in it, a request so humble that it elicits a high success rate among tourists. The most successful beggars are the half-dozen ladino men who post themselves along Insurgentes and Utrilla, and intercept passing pedestrians, either at street corners or in narrow parts of the sidewalk (fig. 9). They almost block passage with an outstretched bowl or plate. They watch oncoming pedestrians, singling out tourists and middle-class ladinos, and obviously graduate their solicitations according to social status. With the affluent, their requests are insistent, and a failure to respond is followed by an indignant rebuke. Every fourth or fifth attempt is successful on the average.

Besides food, lodgings, and handicrafts, tourists also seek information and travel services. The vast majority of tourists, even the ones who come with guided tours where most of the decisions have been made for them, rely on guidebooks and on each other for information, thus limiting the market for the local dispensation of tourist information. This is especially true of the two principal categories of ethnic tourists who come to San Cristóbal. The organized tours are escorted from their Mexican point of departure (frequently Mexico City or Cancún) by a Mexican guide who is not a local and effectively freezes out local guides (fig. 33). The backpack tourists, on the other hand, are by self-definition independent and disinclined to be told what to see, much less to pay for the service (fig. 32).

There is, however, an important free source of local information, the tourist office on the Zócalo, supported by the tourist department of the state of Chiapas. A continuous trickle of tourists seek information or advice there from two articulate and personable young ladinas, one of whom also speaks some English (fig. 31). Most of the customers walk around the office without addressing the employees, and glean information from the maps and posters on the walls and from the multiple hotel, restaurant, and transport advertisements displayed on two centrally located carousels (fig. 30). Many of the advertisements are multilingual (usually in Spanish, English, French, and German). Tourists who address the employees usually make an effort to speak Spanish and are asked to sign a guest book, but they are no more than a fourth or so of those who enter the office, and those, in turn, are a minority of all tourists. (Organized tours make little use of the tourist office, for instance.)

In addition to the state tourist office, half a dozen private travel

---

1. My description is limited to facilities that cater *primarily* to tourists, but tourists also frequent a number of places not principally designed for them. Pharmacies, grocery stores, the post office, telephone offices, the laundromat, and several banks are among the amenities that receive tourists along with locals. In some of them, the tourist presence is quite visible, such as at the foreign exchange window of a major bank on the Zócalo.

agencies and an Avis car rental office also provide information and services to visiting tourists. Half of them are attached to three of the better hotels, and the others are independent. The main service they offer is to book flights, mostly on internal Mexican lines, and to provide local transportation and guides for one- or two-day excursions around San Cristóbal, mostly in chartered microbuses. These services are either locally sought by the tourists themselves or arranged for in advance and subcontracted from larger tourist agencies, in Mexico City, Cancún, Villahermosa, Oaxaca, or other main tourist centers. The travel agencies generally own their own microbuses, but also charter larger buses from local bus owners. In the microbuses, the driver usually serves as guide as well.

Local full-time professional guides are remarkably few. I have met only three whose level of local expertise and knowledge of foreign languages would qualify them as professionals. One is a young German woman who is based in San Cristóbal and contracts with tour agencies from Germany, Austria, and Switzerland to escort organized bus tours for their entire circuit, which typically includes San Cristóbal, but starts or finishes at Cancún or Mexico City. The other two are local ladinos. One is Sergio Castro, an ex-teacher in his forties who spent many years teaching in Indian communities, knows some Tzotzil, and takes a genuine interest in the health, education, and welfare of Indians. A wing of his home is devoted to a small private museum with an excellent regional collection of textiles. He freelances with French-language tour organizers. During the day, he accompanies groups of French, Belgian, Swiss, or Québecois tourists as a guide to Chamula. In the evening, he gives the same groups a tour of his textile collection and a prepared slide show. His French is somewhat limited but adequate to the task. He also uses the opportunity to collect money, school supplies, and medicines from the tourists for distribution to the Indian communities with which he maintains close ties.

The third professional guide is a young woman who used to work in the tourist office and parlayed her fairly fluent English into a specialized service from which she makes a handsome living. She takes small groups of eight to twelve English-speaking tourists (principally Americans, Britons, Germans, Dutch, and Scandinavians) on a "nontypical" walking tour of Chamula and Zinacantán. She charges $9 per person for a six-hour tour, and makes in two days what an average primary school teacher would earn in a month. She claims great expertise of local Indians, but she refused to be interviewed or observed on her tours, possibly threatened by the prospect of my discovering the limits of her expertise. (By contrast, Sergio Castro is completely open and undefensive about his activities.)

Besides these three professional guides, a few young men who act as drivers for the travel agencies also do some guiding. I met another two young men who had managed to attach themselves to small groups of somewhat insecure North American tourists, and who seem to cruise the produce market for prospective customers. The produce market—a crowded, confusing, noisy, and odorous place—is the ideal setting to offer guide services to the independent but somewhat timorous tourists who want to be close to the Indians but fear pickpockets and other lurking hazards. The market is also the departure point of microbuses to the Indian villages, and finding space on the right bus without a knowledge of Spanish is a somewhat intimidating task. The market attracts a few pickpockets as well, but at fairly low densities. I encountered only one victim, a middle-aged Frenchman whose passport and traveler's checks were stolen from a small backpack.

In terms of tourist attractions and "sights," San Cristóbal is not the kind of town that tourists "do," guidebook in hand, following itineraries of "musts." Most tourists seem to view the entire town as a backdrop of colonial quaintness in which to see Indians. The two markets and the Zócalo are the principal venues for people watching. Many tourists will also take a peek at nearby churches, especially the cathedral, Santo Domingo, and La Caridad, but for the most part they cast only a cursory ten- to fifteen-second glance from the door. Two museums charge admission, the private Na Bolom collection ($1.10) and the INAH historical and ethnography museum (40 cents), but together they receive barely 10 percent of the tourist traffic through town. Indeed, the INAH museum, like most state museums in Mexico, has signs in Spanish only, and sees its principal mission as educating the Mexican public rather than attracting tourists. Most visitors are classes of school children escorted by their teachers, who are admitted free of charge.

In addition to being an attraction in its own right, San Cristóbal is also a jumping-off point to nearby attractions, especially to the Indian

villages of Chamula, Zinacantán, Tenejapa, Huistán, Oxchuc, Amatenango, San Andrés, and others, to the lakes of Montebello, to the
nearby caves ten kilometers away, to the Cañon del Sumidero, to the
ruins of Toniná and Palenque, and to the cascades of Agua Azul. All of
these can be reached in a one-day trip from San Cristóbal. Finally, San
Cristóbal, to many, is merely an overnight stopping point on a circuit to
or from Guatemala, the Yucatán Peninsula and Palenque, Villahermosa
and Veracruz, the Isthmus and Oaxaca, or the Pacific Coast resorts.

STATISTICAL TRENDS

5   THE TOURISTS

GENERAL MEXICAN TOURISM

As everyone knows, most of all the Mexican government, tourism is big business. In 1988, the 5.69 million foreign visitors to Mexico brought in $1,349 million more than Mexicans spent abroad. Mexican hotels and restaurants generated some 3 percent of the gross domestic product, and the hospitality industry created 522,000 direct jobs and 1.3 million indirect jobs—affecting roughly 2 percent of the Mexican population and close to one-tenth of the labor force (Hiernaux and Rodríguez 1990). Mexico has long been extremely tourism conscious, and has made enormous investments, both public and private, in promoting tourism. The Secretariat of Tourism is a cabinet-level unit of the federal government, and publishes a vast amount of both promotional literature and "how to" manuals for trainees in the hospitality industry. The locally published literature on tourism, including a recent twenty-volume encyclopedia, is substantial and rapidly growing (Acerenza 1985; Boullon 1985; de la Torre Padilla 1980; Getino 1987; Hiernaux 1989; Molina 1982; Romero 1988).

All levels of government—federal, state, and local—do everything they can to promote tourism. At the federal level, this has taken mostly two forms: first, building and maintaining an ever-improving infrastructure of paved roads, bridges, airports, and other public works in the field of transportation and communications (notably a still insufficient but rapidly improving telephone system); second, developing mammoth planned resorts, principally along the Pacific and Caribbean coasts, such as Acapulco, Manzanillo, Mazatlán, Puerto Vallarta, Ixtapa, Puerto Escondido, Cancún, and now Huatulco. A large federal agency, the Fondo Nacional de Fomento al Turismo (FONATUR), manages credit for investment in the hospitality industry.

At the state level, governments have mostly produced promotional pamphlets for regional attractions, funded tourist information offices in cities, and, in some cases, promoted low-cost bus excursions for schoolchildren, teachers, employees, and other Mexicans of modest means. The latter activity is known as *turismo social*, and is combined with visits to museums and archaeological sites, both of which are heavily patronized by appreciative Mexicans proud of their historical heritage.

Finally, at the local, municipal level, the promotion of tourism has taken mostly the form of private investment in hotels, restaurants, travel agencies, bus companies, and other services, and in municipal efforts (often supervised and subsidized by federal agencies) to preserve and restore colonial architecture and to prevent the construction of modern buildings that would destroy architectonic homogeneity.

According to Secretary of Tourism Pedro Joaquín Coldwell, Mexico receives approximately 1.5 percent of the world's annual international tourist traffic of some 400 million travelers and $150 billion in revenues (Suárez 1990). That translates into some five million foreign visitors to Mexico per year, a figure the Secretary finds lamentably low and hopes to double in five years' time. The trend is clearly upward: in 1949,

Mexico received 323,000 foreign guests; in 1959, 746,000; by 1983, the number had risen to 4,780,000; in 1988, there were 5,690,000 (Hiernaux and Rodríguez 1990). Mexico's principal promotional effort has been directed at North America and at the development of coastal resorts. Over 90 percent of tourists come from North America (86 percent from the United States, 5 percent from Canada), and an equal percentage of the tourist trade is of the "sun-sand-and-sea" variety— that is, centering on the coastal resorts (Suárez 1990). In fact, these coastal resorts now constitute such self-contained tourist ghettos that they can almost be considered a special region of Mexico, aptly called "Club Mex" by Casagrande (1988). Not all North Americans work exclusively on their suntans, but there is a close association between these two figures: the vast bulk of Mexican tourism is coastal in destination and North American in origin. Winter is the high season.

However, the federal government is increasingly conscious of a growing cultural tourism, all the more so as it peaks during the summer months, thus helping to boost year-round hotel occupancy rates. Cultural tourists come principally from Western Europe and, in recent years, in growing numbers from Japan. The federal government is currently promoting two cultural circuits: one of twelve colonial cities, mostly in the center of the country, and the Ruta Maya in the southeast, of which San Cristóbal is a part.

Using the five million annual figure for foreign tourists as a base, foreign cultural tourism accounts for a yearly flow of approximately half a million (10 percent of the total). However, two factors greatly increase these figures. One is the great importance of domestic tourism. According to the statistics cited by the Secretary of Tourism, domestic tourism is six times greater than international tourism (some thirty million travelers a year), and accounts for 70 percent of revenues of Mexican hotels (Suárez 1990). Assuming that the proportion of Mexican vacationers who are primarily cultural tourists is roughly the same 10 percent as for foreign tourists, we can estimate the total cultural tourism flow at between three and four million a year. The second factor to be taken into account is that cultural tourists, especially the foreign ones, spend more time on their vacations than the typical one-to-two-week, sun-sand-and-sea tourist. Thus, in terms of hotel nights, this representation may well be twice or more the 10 percent suggested by their numbers. The data of the present study are especially telling on this point: 14 percent of the foreign tourists in the San Cristóbal sample had spent three or more months in Mexico on their current vacation, and 65 percent, more than a month.

TOURISM IN SAN CRISTÓBAL

Turning to local tourist office statistics, Table 1 shows the annual flow of Mexicans and foreigners who stayed for at least one night in San Cristóbal. Approximately 543,000 visitors passed through in the four years immediately prior to the study (1986–89), for an annual average of 136,000. Approximately 56 percent of that traffic consisted of Mexicans. If we are to believe the figure that, at the national level, Mexican tourists outnumber foreign ones by six to one, then they are underrepresented in San Cristóbal. In fact, they are probably *undercounted.* Many stay with friends or relatives, and thus do not appear in hotel figures on which local statistics are based. Furthermore, many are school groups or families coming on day trips from neighboring towns such as Tuxtla and Comitán.

The possibility also exists, however, that an even smaller percentage of Mexican travelers are cultural tourists than the 10 percent of foreign tourists who can be classified as such. Another problem is that, with Mexicans, the definition of who is a tourist is more problematic than with foreigners. Is the local schoolchild who visits a museum or an archaeological site on a school outing to be counted as a tourist? (The example is not trivial, for schoolchildren make up most of the admissions to the San Cristóbal INAH historical museum, and a decision either to include or exclude them can profoundly affect conclusions.) Whether the 56 percent figure for national tourism in San Cristóbal is an underestimate, as it may well be, it is clear that, in the present study, Mexicans are even more underrepresented (a mere 11 out of our sample of 175). This study must be regarded principally as one of *foreign* tourism, although even the small number of Mexican tourists reveals rather important differences between Mexican and foreign tourists.

As Table 1 shows, nearly a quarter million foreign tourists (245,335) passed through San Cristóbal between 1986 and 1989 (four years).

Table 1

Tourists Who Stayed in San Cristóbal at Least One Night,
by Year and Nationality

Year	Mexicans	Foreigners	Total
1986	70,286	40,026	110,312
1987	79,944	62,530	142,474
1988	76,143	72,147	148,290
1989	71,668	70,632	142,300
Total	298,041	245,335	543,376

Source: San Cristóbal tourist office.

Dividing that figure by four, and relating it to the annual flow of a half-million foreign cultural tourists, we can deduce that perhaps one foreigner in eight who is interested in Mexican culture passes through San Cristóbal.

San Cristóbal is clearly a well-established stopping point on several itineraries, meriting at least an overnight stay. It acquired a reputation on the cultural tourist circuit for being one of the prettiest colonial small towns in Mexico (with only the distant Pátzcuaro and Taxco as rivals), the center of the most authentically Indian area of Mexico, and the heart of a scenic mountainous area endowed with a mild climate of "perpetual spring." In the words of one guidebook among many: "San Cristóbal . . . is a colonial city set in a lovely valley. (Note: It's chilly every evening of the year there, so bring a sweater.) The town is the major market center for Indians of various tribes from the surrounding mountains, chiefly the Chamulas, who wear baggy thigh-length trousers and white or black serapes. . . . In a way, Indian life in Chiapas is an introduction to that of Guatemala, for San Cristóbal is deep in Mesoamerica where the Mayas flourished" (Brosnahan and Kretchman 1977:312).

The two nearest towns of any size are Comitán, 100 kilometers to the east, and the state capital of Tuxtla, 85 kilometers to the west. Neither approaches the historical interest, physical attractiveness, and tourist amenities of San Cristóbal, and Tuxtla has a hot, humid climate without offering the compensating attraction of being a coastal resort. San Cristóbal is the obvious choice to stop, rest, and sightsee within a 100 kilometer radius in all directions. Basically, San Cristóbal is a stopover on a limited number of itineraries which include: (1) travelers to and from Guatemala, following the Pan-American Highway; (2) the Ruta Maya tourists who often start and finish their circuit in Cancún or Mérida, and visit the principal Maya sites of Chichén Itzá, Uxmal, Tulum, and Palenque; and (3) those on a Mexican grand tour which begins and/or ends in Mexico City or Cancún, and typically includes a mixture of archaeological sites (principally in Yucatán), colonial cities (especially Puebla and Oaxaca), and coastal resorts either on the Pacific Coast or on the Caribbean.

SEASONALITY AND FLOW

One important question my sample cannot answer is that of seasonality of the tourist flow, since all interviews were conducted during the winter months. Here the tourist office statistics are especially useful. The flow of arrivals is continuous, with the lowest months (May, June, September, October, and November) averaging slightly under half the highest months (March, April, July, August, and December). The peak three months of 1989, for instance, show 19,642 arrivals in August, 15,107 in July, and 15,929 in March, compared to 7,434 in September, 8,350 in June, and 8,105 in May, the lowest three months. The three peak periods correspond to vacation periods: the Christmas–New Year vacation in the second half of December, which attracts mostly Mexicans and North Americans; the summer vacation months of July and August, when the flow is mostly Europeans who come on longer trips; and Holy Week, the week preceding the movable feast of Easter, when the Mexican middle class travels in droves.

Converted to a daily basis, these tourist statistics (which may underestimate the actual flow by perhaps 10 percent) mean that San Cristóbal receives some 500 to 650 new visitors a day during peak months, and 200 to 300 during the low months. With a hotel capacity of some 440 rooms (overwhelmingly double rooms), these figures translated into occupancy rates ranging from a high of 72 percent in August to a low of 31 percent in June, with a monthly average of 48 percent in 1989. The 1988 monthly average was nearly identical: 49 percent.

The above daily figures substantially understate the actual number of tourists physically present in San Cristóbal on any given day, however, since the average stay in town exceeds one day. Foreign tourists stayed for an average of 1.6 days and Mexicans for 1.4 days, for a combined mean of 1.5 days. Thus the peak figures of tourists present in town in the summer months average 750 to 1,000, while the off-season months average 300 to 450. The more visible foreigners make up between half and three-fourths of these numbers, depending on the season.

SAMPLE CHARACTERISTICS

Let me now turn to a statistical profile of my nonrandom sample of 175 tourists, chosen according to the criteria described in Chapter 2. Each of them was interviewed, following an open-answer schedule which could, when rushed, be administered in twelve to fifteen minutes, but which, in nearly all cases, took from twenty to sixty minutes. On all items, tourists were left free to answer in their own words rather than asked to choose between preordained categories or scales. Whenever possible, I shall compare my sample with the more comprehensive but less detailed information recorded in the tourist office. As noted in Chapter 2, both sources of data have some biases. The two main categories of tourists underrepresented in my sample are Mexicans (because they blend more into the local scene and are less easy to identify unequivocally as tourists), and, possibly, organized tour customers (because they are much more in a hurry, have to keep up with the group, and thus are more difficult to interview). The official statistics, on the other hand, tend to underrepresent tourists who pass through without spending the night in San Cristóbal, and those who either camp, stay in private homes, or rent rooms in cheap posadas. Some of these missed by the tourist office, however, were captured in my sample. With the two exceptions just noted, my sample, though small, is probably representative of visitors, especially foreign visitors, to San Cristóbal.

Table 2 gives the distribution by age and sex. The slightly greater number of men in the sample is probably due to the bias of the man volunteering to be the subject when I approached a couple, thereby foiling my attempt to interview an equal number of men and women. (This was especially evident in the case of Mexican tourists.) Perhaps

Table 2

*Tourists in Study Sample Visiting in San
Cristóbal, by Age and Sex (N = 175)*

Age	Male	Female	Total
15–19	1	2	3
20–24	13	16	29
25–29	24	15	39
30–34	20	9	29
35–39	9	5	14
40–44	13	2	15
45–49	3	5	8
50–54	3	6	9
55–59	4	3	7
60–64	6	3	9
65–69	4	4	8
70–74	1	2	3
75 +	1	1	2
Total	102	73	175

the most salient feature in this table is that ethnic tourists tend to be young adults between twenty and thirty-four years of age. Over half (55 percent) of the sample fall in that fifteen-year interval. An additional 17 percent are between thirty-five and forty-four, which means that nearly three-fourths (72 percent) are under forty-five. Younger and older age groups are underrepresented. (I arbitrarily excluded children from my sample, my youngest respondent being a tall fifteen-year-old, but I did seek to sample older people.) Of the 175 adults interviewed, only 11 (6 percent) were accompanied by children, usually only one or two of them. Ethnic tourists are primarily young adults in the prime of life and unencumbered by children.

Table 3 shows the sample characteristics in terms of nationality and occupation. A total of nineteen nationalities are represented (some were lumped into regional categories when the numbers were fewer than three). The sample has relatively few Mexicans and French, and more Americans and Swiss than the tourist office statistics, but generally the national origins of tourists are quite comparable in both data sets.

Table 3

Tourists in Study Sample Visiting San Cristóbal by Nationality and Occupation
(N = 175)

Nationality	Professional (Univ. Educ.)	Business and Managerial	White-collar Technical	Students (University)	Manual Worker	Homemaker	Other	Total
Mexican	6	1	2	1	1	0	0	11
American (U.S.)	19	12	6	4	4	2	3	50
German	8	1	12	6	6	0	0	33
French	5	2	9	1	0	3	1	21
Swiss	2	1	5	1	6	1	0	16
Canadian	5	2	1	2	2	1	1	14
Italian	0	1	0	0	3	0	0	4
British	2	1	1	0	0	0	0	4
Scandinavian	0	0	2	1	2	0	0	5
Dutch	1	1	1	0	0	0	0	3
Austrian	0	0	2	0	1	0	0	3
Other European	1	2	1	1	0	0	0	5
Japanese	0	0	0	3	0	0	0	3
Latin American	1	0	0	0	1	0	0	2
Australian	0	0	1	0	0	0	0	1
Total	50	24	43	20	26	7	5	175

Seasonality accounts for the differences: European visitors come disproportionately during the summer months, especially August, when
the town is awash in French and German tour buses; North Americans
are relatively more in evidence during the winter months, when this
study was made. Nearly all (96 percent of the sample; 94 percent of the
tourist office statistics) came from Mexico itself, the United States,
Canada, and Western Europe. About two-thirds (66 percent of the
sample; 60 percent of the tourist office statistics) come from four countries: Mexico, the United States, France, and Germany, though not
necessarily in that order. Eighty-nine percent of my sample spoke one
of only four languages—English, Spanish, French, and German—as
their mother tongue, and *all* of them spoke at least one of these languages, and not infrequently several, as second languages. As is true
of other forms of tourism as well, ethnic tourism is largely a First-

to-Third-World and a North-to-South phenomenon: it consists overwhelmingly of people from rich, cold, northern, capitalist countries
coming to poor, warm, southern, peripheral countries. Only in recent
years is the flow of West Europeans and North Americans beginning to
be augmented by Japanese, as well as the elite of the Third World and a
sprinkle from the Second World. (My sample, for instance, included
two Hungarians who had flown to Mexico via East Berlin and Havana.)

This privileged origin of ethnic tourists is further confirmed by
the occupational distribution in my sample. Three high status groups
(university-educated professionals, businessmen and managers, and
university students) make up well over half (54 percent) of my sample,
compared to one-fourth (25 percent) for the white-collar, semiprofes-
sional, technical middle class, and a bare 15 percent for the working
class. Furthermore, it must be noted that traveling for pleasure, insofar
as it is an option for the working class at all, is almost entirely limited to
the working class of *affluent* countries. Eight out of the eleven Mexican
tourists in our sample (73 percent) belong to the three privileged categories, and the one worker was really not a tourist. (See Chapter 2.) By
comparison, only 1.5 percent of economically active men in the state of
Chiapas in 1980 belonged to the professional and managerial elite.
Mexican tourists are clearly not a cross section of the population!

Table 3 thus clearly shows that tourism in general, and probably even
more so ethnic tourism, is very much an elite phenomenon largely
restricted to the more educated, wealthier people from the rich countries. Ethnic tourism, then, consists largely of rich, university-trained
people coming to look at poor, mostly illiterate peasants, who, inciden-
tally, made up nearly three-fourths (74 percent) of the population of
Chiapas in 1980.

EXPENDITURES

How much time do tourists spend in Mexico, and how much money
do they spend per day? Table 4 gives us the picture. Length of stay
ranged from a few days to over a year, excluding, of course, the eleven
Mexican tourists to whom the question did not apply. The surprising
finding was how long the sample stayed in Mexico. Almost two-thirds

Table 4

Length of Stay in Mexico and Daily Expenditures of San Cristóbal Tourists
(N = 175)

U.S. $ per day	<10	10–14	15–19	20–24	25–29	30–39	40–49	50–59	60–89	90+	N/A	Total
<5	0	0	0	0	0	0	0	1	1	2	0	4
5–9	0	0	0	2	0	3	0	0	1	6	0	12
10–14	1	0	2	5	2	8	4	1	12	6	2	43
15–19	0	0	3	4	1	7	2	1	7	1	0	26
20–24	0	1	2	3	2	5	1	1	5	2	1	23
25–29	1	1	1	5	1	2	0	0	0	1	0	12
30–34	0	0	1	2	1	1	0	0	0	2	1	8
35–39	0	0	0	0	0	2	2	1	1	2	2	10
40–49	1	1	0	0	1	2	0	0	0	0	0	5
50–59	0	0	1	0	0	2	0	1	2	0	0	6
60+	0	5	2	4	0	5	0	0	0	1	1	18
No Reply	1	1	0	0	0	0	2	0	0	0	4	8
Total	4	9	12	25	8	37	11	6	29	23	11	175

(65 percent) of the foreign tourists stay over a month; nearly one-third (32 percent) stay over two months; one in seven (14 percent) stays over three months. These figures are, in fact, underestimates of time spent on the current trip, because over half of the sample (53 percent) spent additional time in other countries on the same trip. Clearly, we are dealing here with a young group that enjoys a lot of leisure, another mark of elite status and privilege. Our sample stayed in Mexico much longer than the average foreign tourist, who, in 1987, was spending an average of 9.7 days in the country (Hiernaux and Rodríguez 1990).

As for expenditures, there, too, the range was quite large: the most parsimonious spend only $2 a day, while at the other end of the scale, some pay as much as $200 for guided tours.[1] The range between low-budget travelers and splurgers is thus an astonishing one hundred to

---

1. For the sake of constancy, most prices here are given in U.S. dollars. The study was done when the U.S. dollar was worth some 2,700 pesos, but, as the peso sinks rapidly in value, peso figures would quickly become obsolete. Daily expenditures include neither the cost of transportation to Mexico nor purchases

one. Also interesting is that the mode and the mean are close to the low end of the distribution. The $10–$14 category is the modal one, and, excluding the eight "no replies," nearly two-thirds (65 percent) of the sample spend less than $25 a day; over four-fifths (83 percent) spend less than $40. This is well below the 1987 average daily expenditure of $43 for foreign visitors to Mexico (Hiernaux and Rodríguez 1990). Fifteen of eighteen people in the "over $60" category are guided tour members who in fact were spending well over $100 a day on the average.

What we have, then, is a bimodal distribution with about one-tenth of the sample who travel in organized groups and spend over $100 a day, and a four-fifths majority that averages around $15 to $20, with a huge gap in between. The situation is made even more interesting by the negative correlation ($r = -.34$) between length of time in Mexico and amount spent per day, and the fairly strong positive correlation ($r = +.54$) between age and amount spent. We have, in fact, two tourist clienteles here: many leisured young people spending a lot of time but relatively little money, and traveling independently; and fewer, older people staying for shorter periods, traveling in organized tours, and spending much more. These two groups are clearly recognized in local San Cristóbal culture as the backpack and guided-tour tourists respectively.

MEXICAN VERSUS FOREIGN TOURISTS

Later, we shall deal with the implications of this dichotomy for tourist-host perceptions and interaction. On the whole, ethnic tourists are not big spenders; in fact, they often travel in a style of consumption well below their customary one at home, and are frequently perceived by their hosts as much poorer than they in fact are. *Turismo pobre* is a common local characterization of ethnic tourists by middle-class Mexi-

---

other than of food, lodging, and internal transportation in Mexico. Daily expenditures are mostly the best estimates of what respondents thought they spent per day, per person, over the entire trip, not including transportation to Mexico.

cans, who themselves travel more lavishly and have difficulty understanding why foreigners might want to travel "below their class."

Even when playing at being poor, however, the ethnic tourist is in a highly privileged situation. First, parsimony is often a matter of choice rather than necessity. Second, even when spending "only," say, $15 a day, the tourist still devotes to his or her amusement something like four or five times the wages of a Mexican rural laborer. An entertainment budget which is four times the subsistence income of a peasant family of five or more people represents, in fact, extreme leisure and luxury by local standards. Third, the main luxury commodity consumed by ethnic tourists, no matter how limited their budget, is the freedom from want which makes so much unproductive leisure time available. Living frugally while traveling is simply part of the tourism experience away from the materialism and consumerism of home. Economical travel is a way of being "closer to the people"—that is, part and parcel of the search for authenticity inherent in ethnic tourism.

Tourist office statistics on the average amount spent per day validate the findings of this study. In 1989, Mexican tourists spent $20.22 per day per person in San Cristóbal (using a conversion rate of 2,500 pesos per dollar for 1989), while foreign tourists spent $17.41. These figures replicate almost exactly those from the study sample and are a good indication of the latter's representativeness. What is most interesting about the official statistics, however, is that Mexicans outspend foreigners. Many readers may find this fact counterintuitive, and, indeed, I too would have expected the reverse, until I began to understand the local situation.

To be sure, Mexico is poorer than the countries of most foreign tourists, but in Mexico only the upper and upper-middle class can afford to travel for pleasure. Furthermore, Mexico is a very class-conscious society. It stands to reason that high status, class-conscious Mexicans in their own country carry their status with them, and expect the best services to a greater extent than foreign tourists who cover the entire status range (as we have seen from our sample), who come from countries with less visible class distinctions, and who, being abroad, are not very concerned about the social esteem of their hosts.

As several hoteliers confirmed to me, Mexican tourists are *muy exigentes* ("very demanding"). They expect not only the quality of service

1. *General view of San Cristóbal from the Cerro, near the Zócalo, looking eastward.*

2. *View of San Cristóbal from the Cerro, looking southward.*

3. A quiet residential street, away from the tourist traffic, yet less than 200 meters from Santo Domingo market.

4. *Baroque facade of Santo Domingo church, built in the mid-sixteenth century. This is a major tourist attraction. The adjacent cloister of the ex-Dominican convent now houses the INAH museum and the Na Jolóbil Cooperative.*

5. The statue of Diego de Mazariegos, founder of San Cristóbal, said to be unique in Mexico in honoring a Spanish conquistador. An irreverent note has been added, however: the beer bottle cradled in his left arm.

13. An evening concert of Chamula music on the Zócalo. This was a staged event in connection with the Indian congress, but it was directed at locals, not tourists. As yet, there are no performances of "staged authenticity" directed primarily at tourists.

14. *The village of San Juan Chamula, a major tourist attraction, 12 kilometers from San Cristóbal, at carnival time. A trilingual sign warns tourists against taking pictures of carnival rites on the plaza.*

15. *Chamula children immobilize an incoming car of Mexican tourists, to sell and beg in whining voices. This is a recent response to growing tourist traffic.*

16. *Young Chamula man in charge of tourist office in San Juan Chamula. He sells 1,000 peso (thirty-five cent) tickets to visit the church. Behind him is a quadrilingual sign warning against taking photographs inside the church and at carnival time.*

17. *French tourists buy and try on nontraditional made-for-tourists textiles in San Juan Chamula. Chamula sellers dress tourists in their wares to promote sales.*

18. *A French tourist has just taken a posed photograph of two Chamula men in front of the church. They requested no payment, but he thanked them by giving each of them several cigarettes.*

19. A busy commercial arcade on the Zócalo, frequented by ladinos, Indians, and tourists alike, is on the axis of Avenidas Insurgentes and Utrilla.

20. The busy Santo Domingo craft market around noon. This is the principal meeting ground between tourists and tourees. The sellers are nearly all Chamulas.

21. An unhurried, informally dressed tourist closely inspects a Chamula woman's wares, made up of both Guatemalan imports and local made-for-tourists textiles.

22. A Chamula woman displays her goods inside the patio of the Diego de Mazariegos Hotel, a prime location where most customers pay well above minimum selling prices.

23. Authentic Chiapas textiles for sale at high prices in the Na Jolóbil Cooperative, next to the Church of Santo Domingo.

24. A ladino-owned microbus, strategically parked on Avenida Utrilla, next to Santo Domingo, serves as low-overhead salesroom for leather goods.

25. Lacandones from the Chiapas lowlands have come to San Cristóbal to sell bunches of bows and arrows made for tourists, at 3,000 ($1.10) a bunch.

26. *Indian actors perform in Spanish a locally produced play in the patio of Na Bolom to an audience of local ladinos and resident expatriates. The famous Trudy Blom stands third from left, next to a young man, in the back row. The show was not a tourist performance.*

27. *Attractive tourist accommodations abound in San Cristóbal. Here, La Galería restaurant in a restored colonial house.*

28. *One of the two colonial patios of the Diego de Mazariegos Hotel.*

29. Local upper-class ladinos and resident Americans are eating their Sunday lunch (when their maids have the day off) in the patio of the Ciudad Real Hotel.

30. Tourists inspect advertisements for hotels, restaurants, and other services inside the tourist office. Note Indian photographs and textiles used as wall decorations.

31. A young tourist couple asks for information from a tourist office employee. Note again the prominence of Indians in the wall decorations. The town is obviously marketing "its" Indians.

32. Backpack tourism in action: four young Europeans walk down Avenida Insurgentes, on their way from their hotel to the bus station.

33. Group tourism in action: hotel porters carry suitcases to the tour bus outside, while tour group members do some hurried after-breakfast shopping before leaving for Palenque.

34. Budget campers in the cheap ($3 a night per vehicle) San Nicolás trailer park.

35. A row of ladino-owned tourist shops along Avenida Utrilla, located on the way to the produce market.

36. German tourists shopping for leather belts in a ladino shop along Avenida Utrilla.

37. Where the line between tourist and touree becomes blurred: Chamula street hawkers sell made-for-tourists weavings to other Indians, who came from other parts of Mexico for the PRI-sponsored congress.

38. Where the line between tourist and middleman becomes blurred: the family of vignette 11, Chapter 5. They live from the sale of the costume jewelry they make. The hut behind them is their home.

39. Where the line between tourist and resident becomes blurred: resident gringos go shopping in the produce market.

40. Ladinos selling "living Mayas": a mural of San Juan Chamula in the Hotel D'Monica.

41. *Ladinos marketing dead Mayas: murals inspired by Bonampak paintings in Hotel D'Monica.*

42. *The quintessential touree: Chamula cargo holders at a mass meeting of Indians under PRI auspices.*

43. *The quintessential middlemen: the National President of the PRI and the Governor of Chiapas, dressed up as Zinacantecos, promise the Indians that the government is no longer going to ignore them.*

44. *The quintessential tourist: meeting the other.*

but also the personal attention and class deference to which they are accustomed. Slumming holds no charm for them. One Mexican tourist, for example, described the Hotel Santa Clara, one of the three or four best in San Cristóbal, and the only one with a swimming pool, as *horroroso* ("horrifying"); two stated that San Cristóbal did not, as yet, have a single good hotel; and two others complained about the poor quality of television reception and the absence of a color TV set in the hotel room.

In short, five out of the eleven Mexican tourists I interviewed thought San Cristóbal did not meet their expectations for quality of hotel services, while foreign tourists were overwhelmingly positive in their assessments. Of the thirty-nine people who spontaneously praised the quality of tourist services in San Cristóbal, only one was Mexican. Many Mexicans expect the best, in terms of modern, international-class facilities, while many foreigners, especially ethnic tourists, seek quaintness, basic cleanliness and safety, and good value for the money. The evaluation criteria are very different indeed.

LENGTH OF STAY

Even tourists who spend a lot of time in Mexico stay in San Cristóbal only for a few days. One-tenth (10 percent) pass through in one day without staying overnight; one-fourth (25 percent) stay two days; another fourth (27 percent) stay three days; in sum, over three-fourths (77 percent) stay five days or less. Nearly a tenth (9 percent), however, extend their stay for more than ten days, and a sprinkling stay for months. These length-of-stay figures are somewhat higher than the mean of 1.6 days from the tourist office statistics, but this is probably a function of the fact that the tourist office counts *nights* spent in San Cristóbal, whereas I was counting *days*, thereby adding one day to most stays. A person arriving, say, Sunday noon and leaving Monday afternoon would be counted by the tourist office as having spent one night and by me as having stayed two days in San Cristóbal.

At the high end of the time scale, the definitional problem arises as to when a long-term tourist becomes a resident. I arbitrarily drew the line at six months' residence in San Cristóbal, because I wanted to exclude resident gringos from my study. At first sight, many residents are not easily distinguished from ethnic tourists, except by subtle behavioral clues, and there is some interaction between tourists and foreign residents, especially at a half dozen restaurants and cafés where expatriates "hang out." Nevertheless, resident gringos emphatically reject the label of tourist and want to distance themselves from the transient foreigners.

Drawing the line at five days, a few differences emerge between the three-fourths of "short-timers" and the less transient one-fourth. Long-timers spend less per day, are younger, are more fluent in Spanish, have fewer negative impressions of San Cristóbal, and come more on the recommendation of friends or family members at home. That is, they tend to have known of San Cristóbal before coming to Mexico, and to have planned an extended stay on the strength of someone's enthusiastic endorsement back home. None of these findings are surprising. At the opposite pole are the organized group of tourists who, in most cases, stay in San Cristóbal overnight, are older, spend more, have just heard of San Cristóbal from their tour leader or guidebook, and typically mispronounce the town's name by accenting the first syllable (Crístobal).

MODE OF TRANSPORT

Since San Cristóbal has no commercial airport or railway service, tourists have to come by road. Just over half (51 percent) come by regular public bus, mostly from Guatemala, Tuxtla, or Palenque. Most try to reserve seats on first-class buses if available, but, especially to Palenque, they have to resort to second-class service. Buses are so cheap in Mexico (about 1.5 cents per kilometer) that even parsimonious tourists seldom hitchhike. (Only one respondent said he regularly did.) As might be expected, public bus travel is associated with younger, independent, unhurried, low budget travelers. It is the obvious choice of the backpackers and ethnic tourists. The few tourists who mention having used trains in other parts of Mexico generally report bad experiences. One family, for instance, had its luggage stolen in the Oaxaca railway station, and another described a long Yucatán train ride as a "journey to hell" in a slow, crowded, acutely uncomfortable train. Most bus travelers, on the other hand, are reasonably satisfied with the quality and price of the service.

A much smaller group (10 percent) of tourists in a greater hurry fly into Tuxtla, and then take a bus or taxi to San Cristóbal, less than two hours by road from the airport. Another 30 percent drive themselves, and are divided in equal proportions between those who come in their own car, in a rented car, or in their own recreational vehicle (camper, trailer, or van). Organized tours (8 percent) come in special tour buses that are usually parked overnight in San Cristóbal and transport the tourists on their entire circuit. Finally, a hardy minority (2 percent) travels by motorcycle.

Mode of transport is fairly closely associated with broad types of travelers. Motorcyclists tend to be young, adventuresome, independent, and parsimonious. Most travel alone, but the sample includes a young German family of three. Mexican tourists predominantly use their own private car, but quite a few also travel by public bus or join organized tours. The state of Chiapas, for instance, subsidizes inexpensive bus tours for schoolchildren, which take loads of pupils on three-day, weekend tours from Tuxtla to Palenque and San Cristóbal. The children are always accompanied by several adults, both parents and teachers.

Foreign tourists who drive fall into two distinct categories. Either they are middle-aged, middle-class family groups (couples with or without children) who rent a small-model car for a minimum of about $50 a day, and who therefore tend to spend more than the average ethnic tourist; or they are North American couples, often in their fifties and sixties, who drive their trailer, van, or camper from home, stay in trailer parks (fig. 34), avoid cities (because of the unsuitability of their large vehicles to Mexican urban traffic), and are generally not ethnic tourists. One agency, Caravanas, caters to this kind of tourist by organizing convoys of fifteen to twenty vehicles led by a "wagon master" and closed by a "tailgater," who also doubles as a mechanic. The arrival of one such caravan in a Mexican small town is usually enough to create an instant traffic jam, as many vehicles are too large to take right turns in narrow streets, but most have the good sense to leave their mobile living rooms in the trailer park along the Pan-American Highway, and to come into

Table 5

Tourists Who Stayed in San Cristóbal at Least One Night, by Nationality and Mode of Transport, 1989 (N = 9,864)

Mode of Transport	Mexicans	Foreigners	Total
Bus	898	5,820	6,718
Own car	770	1,256	2,026
Rental car	117	418	535
Tour bus	40	284	324
Air and bus	154	107	261
Total	1,979	7,885	9,864

Source: San Cristóbal tourist office.

town, invariably in blue-uniformed groups, in a smaller vehicle. Caravanas tourists probably come closest to the stereotype of the naive American who looks lost, out of place, and does not speak any Spanish.

Tourist office statistics for 1989 are broadly congruent with those of the sample for mode of transport used, as shown in Table 5. The nearly 10,000 people in these statistics represent only 7 percent of the 142,300 tourists who came to San Cristóbal in 1989, and underrepresent Mexicans, but nevertheless they are comparable to the characteristics of our small sample. Some 68 percent of the people use public buses, compared to 51 percent in our sample, but among Mexicans the percentage of bus travelers was only 45, while among foreigners it was 74. Some 26 percent of the larger group drove in either their own or a rental car, compared to 30 percent in our sample, but the nationality differences are obvious. While 39 percent of the Mexicans drove their own vehicles, only 16 percent of the foreigners did so. Foreigners, on the other hand, accounted for nearly four-fifths of the car rentals.

Tour bus arrivals and the air-bus combination (some 3 percent each) are less frequent in the tourist office statistics than in our sample (10 and 7 percent respectively). These small differences may well be due to seasonal fluctuations, since my study was limited to two months, while the official statistics cover the entire year. In any case, the overall conclusions of my sample are confirmed by the tourist office data: most people come to San Cristóbal by public bus, even more so foreigners than Mexicans. Organized tours are mostly foreign groups. Foreigners rely more on rental cars, while Mexicans drive their own. The official statistics also indicate that, if anything, our sample slightly underrepresents the more affluent who go on guided tours or travel by private vehicle. However, as these official statistics themselves cover only 7 percent of total arrivals in San Cristóbal, they are probably not any less biased than our own, and not too much should be made of relatively small differences in proportions.

ITINERARIES AND DESTINATIONS

To practically all tourists, San Cristóbal is a stop on an itinerary, not a principal destination. Indeed, over half (53 percent) of the sample visited or intended to visit other countries besides Mexico on their current trip. The most frequent choice is Guatemala, a mere 160 kilometers east of San Cristóbal, which was visited by well over a third (37 percent) of the sample. Thirteen percent visited the United States, 10 percent Belice, and another 10 percent other Latin American countries. (The percentages add up to more than 53, because a number of people visited three or more countries.)

It is not surprising that those who visit other countries besides Mexico tend to be younger, to spend less, to travel by bus, and to be unhurried, independent, and adventuresome. This is especially true of those who go to Guatemala, which has the reputation of being riskier, because of guerrilla activities, but cheaper and more colorful than Mexico, and an ethnic tourist's paradise because of its millions of "unspoiled," "real" Indians. A few organized tours, principally French ones, however, do make brief incursions into Guatemala as part of their "Maya circuit."

Within Mexico, tourists in the sample mention a great number of other stops. Most stop in San Cristóbal as part of an itinerary including twelve or more other cities or archaeological sites. Palenque, the nearest (200 km away) major Maya ruin, is most frequently mentioned, but the list typically includes several other archaeological sites such as Chichén Itzá, Uxmal, Tulum, Tula, Teotíhuacan, and Monte Albán; several cities such as Mérida, Villahermosa, Oaxaca, Cuernavaca, Veracruz, Puebla, Guanajuato, Guadalajara, and, of course, Mexico City; one or more coastal resorts, especially Cancún, Puerto Escondido, Puerto Angel,

Isla Mujeres, Cozumel, or Acapulco; and natural attractions such as the Cañon del Sumidero, the cascades of Agua Azul, nearby caves, Popocatepetl, and others. Most travelers who come through San Cristóbal are in fact on a Mexican grand tour that has no single major focus, but includes a mixture of archaeology, colonial architecture, ethnography, scenic beauty, and plain relaxation. There are, however, some whose main interests are more specific, such as hiking, mountain climbing, Maya archaeology, colonial churches, pottery, weaving, bird watching, river rafting, ecotourism, and so on, but they are a small minority of well under 10 percent.

HOW TOURISTS HEARD OF SAN CRISTÓBAL

One of the standard questions of the interview was where the respondent had first heard of San Cristóbal. Some 9 percent of the sample answered either that they had not heard of the town before coming (mostly organized tour or Caravanas travelers) or that they did not remember because they had always known of it (mostly Mexicans). Excluding these two categories, one-third (34 percent) learned of it either through their tour leader or through a guidebook, and a little over one-third (36 percent) first heard of San Cristóbal through a friend or relative at home who had been there and recommended a visit. Slightly under one-fifth (19 percent) came on the recommendation of other tourists on their current trip, and 8 percent heard of the town through Mexicans in other parts of Mexico.

From these figures, the importance of word-of-mouth recommendation from earlier visitors is evident. Only a third of the sample came because of what they read in guidebooks, although almost all tourists relied on guidebooks for additional information. Most learned about San Cristóbal from others, including other tourists. Ethnic tourists, especially the ones traveling independently, who constantly have to make decisions about where to go next and how, are eager consumers of verbal information. The search for information begins at home before departure but continues on the road with both other tourists and natives. Ethnic tourists are often critical of guidebooks as being insufficient, inaccurate, or out of date. This is especially true for rapidly changing or hard-to-get but vital information, such as bus schedules, the quality of service in small hotels and restaurants, the opening hours of museums and shops, money exchange rates and regulations, and prices of artifacts.

WHAT TOURISTS FIND ATTRACTIVE

When asked what attracted them to San Cristóbal, tourists averaged 1.65 responses per person. Well over half (55 percent) spontaneously mentioned Indians and their cultural products (such as textiles and other handicrafts), thereby confirming San Cristóbal's position as a center of *ethnic* tourism. The second most common reply was the colonial architecture and atmosphere of the town (mentioned by 29 percent, or only half as many as listed Indians as an attraction). A little over one-fifth (21 percent) spoke of the authenticity of San Cristóbal as "picture-book Mexico" or "just my image of what a Mexican town should look like," or simply "the real Mexico," without specifying whether their comment applied to people or buildings, Indians or ladinos. Slightly fewer (19 percent) said that San Cristóbal was on their way to other places, such as Palenque or Guatemala, or expressed admiration for the natural beauty of the region (18 percent). Finally, 10 percent liked the climate, referring mostly to a relief from hot weather in the lowlands. (But a few tourists found San Cristóbal "freezing cold.") Again, the percentages add up to more than 100 because of multiple responses.

The overall picture is quite clear: tourists come to San Cristóbal, first and foremost, because it is at the center of the largest and least westernized Indian area of Mexico, and because its markets and surrounding villages are good places to see Indians and to buy their handicrafts, mostly homespun textiles. They also come because of the quaintness and authenticity of the town itself, but this is only an added bonus to the main attraction for many tourists. Even if one only looks at the tourists' *first* response to the question of what attracted them to San Cristóbal, the Indians "beat" the town by a margin of almost two to one (59 versus 32 first choices).

Yet it is also clear from the multiple responses to the question that, in the aggregate, what makes San Cristóbal such a magnet of ethnic tourism is the combination of Indians, colonial architecture, a sunny, temperate climate, and beautiful mountain scenery. San Cristóbal, in short, has almost everything that a Mexican town can offer, except a major local archaeological site. In the words of a French tourist, San Cristóbal is "le Mexique profond," the authentic Mexican town close to its Maya roots, and where the colonial past still lives, all in a beautiful setting, a pleasant climate, and with a wide choice of cute little hotels and decent restaurants at extremely reasonable prices. It is, in short, an ethnic tourist's dream come true.

WITH WHOM TOURISTS TRAVEL

Tourists were next asked with whom they were traveling. Eighteen percent travel alone, 24 percent with a spouse, 22 percent with a single friend of the opposite sex, 9 percent with a same-sex friend, 6 percent with a spouse and children, 6 percent with other relatives, 2 percent with two or more friends of either sex, 4 percent with acquaintances met on the road, and 9 percent with a tour group. (Some of the latter also traveled with a spouse, relative, or friend, but were classified in the "tour" category to avoid double counting.) Ethnic tourism is to a large extent an activity engaged in by family groups and/or with sexual partners. Excluding the tour groups, and assuming that those traveling with one opposite-sex companion are lovers, about two-thirds (64 percent) of the sample traveled with relatives, sexual partners, or both. (Probably not *all* opposite-sex pairs were sexual partners, but the vast majority were, as indeed were at least two of the same-sex dyads.) Not surprising, married couples, with or without children, were older than the rest of the sample, and spent more per day (excluding the guided tour category). Conversely, solitary travelers and those who travel with nonrelatives tend to be young backpackers.

SIGHTS VISITED

When asked what or whom they had seen or intended to see in and around San Cristóbal, the tourists gave a mean of 2.88 answers each.

The Santo Domingo craft market came in first place; 59 percent of the sample had visited it. It is clearly the centerpiece of a tourist visit to San Cristóbal. Many come to buy artifacts, but the sellers, too, are a main attraction in their own right (figs. 20, 21, 44). They consist overwhelmingly of Chamula women and young children, and are eagerly photographed. In addition, the market stretches between two of the most beautiful colonial churches in town, and near two textile cooperatives and the historical museum (figs. 4, 23). Most tourists come to the market, however, to see Indians and to buy their handicrafts. The Indian village of San Juan Chamula was the second most frequently visited sight; 44 percent had been there or intended to go (figs. 14, 15, 16, 17, 18).

The other sights or activities in descending order of frequency were colonial churches (overwhelmingly Santo Domingo and La Caridad, next to the craft market), mentioned by 37 percent (fig. 4); the produce market, 22 percent (fig. 39); "walking around town," 22 percent; tourist facilities such as hotels and restaurants, 19 percent (figs. 22, 27, 28, 29, 33); the Indian village of Zinacantán, 19 percent; the museum of Na Bolom, 15 percent (fig. 26); the Zócalo, 11 percent (figs. 7, 8, 19, 37); and other Indian villages, 10 percent. Responses of less than 10 percent included in descending order the nearby caves, shopping, "Indians," and the historical museum.

Several patterns emerge clearly from these responses. If one treats the two markets and Na Bolom as places that are attractive primarily because of the presence of Indians and their crafts, then the "Indian" responses account for 60 percent of the total (300 responses out of 504), another confirmation of San Cristóbal as a center of *ethnic* tourism. Combining the responses "Zócalo," "walked around town," and "colonial churches" as an expression of an interest in the town itself and its architecture, these categories add up to less than a fourth (24 percent) of all responses, well under half as many as the "Indian" responses. Naturally, there was considerable overlap in interest between the two broad categories: a large minority of tourists were interested in both, but many more in Indians than in the colonial town.

Another measure of the relative attraction of the two is the number of visitors to Na Bolom, a small private museum featuring mostly Indian arts and crafts, and to the government historical museum, a much larger and better presented set of exhibits, showing both Indian textiles upstairs and an historical exhibit downstairs. Even though the entrance fee to Na Bolom ($1.10) is three times what the state museum charges (40 cents), Na Bolom is mentioned five times more frequently than the state museum. I confirmed the difference by checking on the paid admissions to both museums (excluding schoolchildren, who are freely admitted to both). Na Bolom received some fifty to sixty visitors a day; the state museum admitted an average of twenty-one visitors a day during an eight-day period in February. In addition, another private museum, that owned by Sergio Castro, is probably visited by nearly as many tourists (overwhelmingly French guided tours) as is Na Bolom. It also features almost exclusively Indian artifacts, especially textiles.

CRAFT PURCHASES

The next question on the interview schedule concerned purchases of artifacts. Twenty-two percent of the sample had not bought any in San Cristóbal, nor intended to do so; 14 percent had not yet done so, but said they probably would; the remaining 64 percent did make local purchases of handicrafts, overwhelmingly textiles (both local and Guatemalan), but also leather goods, pottery, small toys, and other souvenirs. Equally interesting was the amount of money tourists spent on craft purchases. This ranged from a low of 25 cents to a high of $5,000. At the low end, 44 percent of those who bought anything spent $10 or less, mostly on very popular but nontraditional belts ($1.10 to $1.50 each) and bracelets (5 to 30 cents each), braided and sold by Chamula women and girls in the market and in the streets (figs. 20, 21, 22, 37). Another 28 percent spent between $11 and $50, and 29 percent spent more than that. Indeed, 5 percent spent over $500. They were, in fact, buying for resale, either on their own behalf or for a relative, and were combining ethnic tourism with a purchasing trip for profit. Not surprising, older (and presumably richer) tourists tended to buy more than younger ones. (The correlation between age and amount purchased is $r = +.30$.)

These purchase figures are, in every case, tourists' estimates, and are only approximate. Some tourists were not finished buying when interviewed, a fact I confirmed when I met several of them later. Furthermore, big buyers tended to forget some of their purchases and to underestimate what they paid. Wives tended to do most of the buying, and, in the presence of their husbands, probably understated their purchases as well. In short, our statistics are likely to be underestimates. Still, it is possible to extrapolate conservatively from them to reach an estimate of the money put in daily circulation through the sale of handicrafts, postcards, souvenirs, and so on, to tourists in San Cristóbal. Assuming that some 65 percent of tourists made such purchases at an average of $20, we arrive at daily expenditures of some $5,000. Multiplying $20 by 65 percent of the 142,300 tourists who passed through San Cristóbal in 1989, the considerable annual sum of $1,850,000 results. Upward rounding to $2,000,000 may still be an underestimate. For example, the largest cooperative estimated its annual gross sales at $130,000, and a large tourist shop at $25,000. To be sure, each was the largest in its class, but, even combined, it is doubtful that they accounted for as much as 8 percent of the estimated total sales of several hundred outlets. Naturally, not all of it is profit, and the benefits are shared by many hundreds of persons. Nevertheless, the monetary impact of such purchases on what would otherwise be a poor, agricultural economy is considerable.

To the $2,000,000 for craft purchases we must add expenditures on tourist services, mostly hotel rooms and meals, but also other purchases such as film, toiletries, pharmaceuticals, laundry, postage, telephone calls, and so on. Using the tourist office statistics of $20.22 for the 71,668 Mexican tourists who came in 1989, and $17.41 for the 70,632 foreigners in the same year, we come to another $2,679,000—again, a conservative figure that can be confidently rounded upward to $3,000,000. In short, tourism brings in about $5,000,000 a year to the San Cristóbal economy. Since nearly all hotels, restaurants, and other tourist facilities are locally owned, money spent in San Cristóbal stays in San Cristóbal, and much of it trickles down to thousands of people. The other side of the tourist bonanza, of course, is that its benefits go disproportionately to a few hundred merchants, hoteliers, and restaurateurs directly involved in the industry, and to a few hundred more of their employees. On a per capita basis, assuming that San Cristóbal has about 100,000 inhabitants, the $5,000,000 translates to only an additional $50 a year. Measured against the Mexican per capita income of some $2,000 a year, the figure seems puny, but the state of Chiapas is much poorer than average. If tourism adds, on average, $250 to the annual income of a local family of five, its contribution is appreciable.

Tourists were also asked about their positive and negative impressions. The former greatly outnumbered the latter. On the average, respondents listed 2.3 positive and 1.4 negative impressions. The most common category of praise concerned what might broadly be called physical environmental conditions: climate, purity of the air, the blue sky, the beautiful mountain scenery, cleanliness, lack of urban pollution and congestion, and the like. Such comments were made by nearly half (48 percent) of the sample. Next most frequent were positive comments about cultural diversity, and the colorful dress and crafts of the Indians, mentioned by 41 percent. The moral and personal qualities of local people, especially their friendliness and hospitality, came in third position with 40 percent, followed by liking for the quaint, peaceful, restful, colonial atmosphere of San Cristóbal as a "typical" Mexican town (35 percent). In fifth place came praise for the unspoiled, authentic character of San Cristóbal as a real, untouristy Mexican town (27 percent). Finally, 22 percent commented favorably on the quality of tourist services, mostly hotels and restaurants, finding them clean, safe, comfortable, and cheap.

By my somewhat subjective judgment, I rated 30 percent of the sample as having strongly positive impressions of San Cristóbal. Those were people who used superlatives and described the town as their favorite in Mexico, a dream picture come true, and so on. Of the rest, I classified 65 percent as moderately positive in their impressions, and 5 percent as slightly positive.

Negative criticisms were not only fewer than the positive ones, they also tended to be much more specific and trivial, and, indeed, in some cases, to apply more to Mexico in general than to San Cristóbal in particular. Almost one-fifth (19 percent) of the sample had some complaints about tourist services, but they tended to be both specific and relatively trivial, such as long queues for changing money in banks, overcrowding of buses, lack of warm water in hotels, slow service in restaurants, and the like. The next most frequent criticism (made by 18 percent) was that San Cristóbal was too "touristy" for their taste, that it was beginning to get "spoiled" by tourism. (One and a half times as many people thought it was *not* touristy yet.)

Tying for third place (17 percent each) were critical comments about the environment (particularly urban pollution in large Mexican cities, perceived lack of concern for environmental degradation, and indiscriminate littering and dumping of garbage along roads), and distress at social conditions (especially poverty, prevalence of disease, child labor, unemployment, and lack of social, educational, and health services for the people). Twelve percent of the sample reported a bad experience in Mexico, mostly *not* in San Cristóbal: there were seven reported cases of theft, five of dishonesty (three of being cheated at Pemex gas stations), three of sexual harassment or "machismo," and five of discourteous, disruptive, or corrupt behavior of the army or police in such situations as roadblocks for drug control, or extortion of a bribe for an alleged traffic violation. In addition, one person was involved in a motorcycle accident and another fell seriously ill.

The last category of critical comments was made up of a sensitive, self-critical 9 percent of the sample who blamed themselves for their uncomfortable or distressed feelings about Mexico. Some, mostly Germans and Scandinavians, felt guilty about their relative wealth, or were shocked by the lack of sensitivity of tourists toward Indians, whom they felt were being treated like animals in a zoo, being stared at and photographed. Others blamed their discomfort or unease on their lack of knowledge of Spanish or some other shortcoming in themselves.

Overall, the bad impressions were relatively mild. I rated only 4 percent of the sample as strongly negative, and 23 percent as moderately negative. The probability of having a bad experience tended to rise slightly with length of stay in Mexico, but, nevertheless, long-term visitors to San Cristóbal were most positive about the town. Of the negative impressions, nearly one-third (31 percent) referred to other parts of Mexico, not to San Cristóbal. Indeed, 40 percent of the sample spontaneously compared San Cristóbal to other places. Of those, over three-fourths (77 percent) preferred San Cristóbal to other places in Mexico. Some declared San Cristóbal to be the best town in Mexico.

Many contrasted the town favorably in relation to the pollution and congestion of Mexico City, or the touristy nature of the coastal resorts, frequently using Cancún and Acapulco as examples of tourism at its nadir. The 14 percent who compared San Cristóbal unfavorably with other places all mentioned Guatemala as cheaper, more authentic, and less touristy. (The remaining 9 percent compared San Cristóbal *both* favorably with other places in Mexico and unfavorably with Guatemala.) In summary, then, ethnic tourists are favorably impressed with San Cristóbal in relation to the rest of Mexico, but find Guatemala even more colorful, attractive, and "untouched."

KNOWLEDGE OF SPANISH

Another important dimension of the tourist experience is fluency in the host country's language. Discounting the eleven Mexican tourists who, not surprisingly, were quite fluent in Spanish, 23 percent of the sample spoke "no" Spanish; 27 percent spoke "little" Spanish; 39 percent spoke "some" Spanish; and 11 percent were "fluent" in it. (These rough categories were assigned either from self-assessment or inferred by observation.) Interestingly, there was no perceptible increase in knowledge of Spanish by length of stay in Mexico, although the repeat visitors to Mexico, and the few long-term visitors to San Cristóbal, were more fluent. A few of the younger, long-term tourists had spent a couple of weeks in a language school (mostly in Guatemala) or intended to do so. Many ethnic tourists make an effort to learn the language of the host country. Most of the foreign tourists whom I observed in the tourist office, for instance, addressed the employees in Spanish. As for the resident gringos, they use their fluency in Spanish as their main asset to distinguish themselves from tourists. Those fluent in Spanish are proud of the fact and delight in displaying their proficiency.

OTHER TRAVEL EXPERIENCES

One final item concerned other travel experiences. The sample is well traveled. Not only are many respondents on the road for a long time;

many are also repeat travelers to Mexico and to other parts of the world. Only 13 percent were on their first trip far away from home (defined as outside Europe for Europeans, and outside North America for Americans, Canadians, or Mexicans). Well over a fourth (28 percent) could be described as habitual travelers, taking a long trip once a year or more. In one extreme case, a person had been nearly continuously globe-trotting for five years, another for three years, and half a dozen for a full year. Forty-four percent had taken between two and nine other long trips abroad. Naturally, the older tended to be the most well traveled. People who take the longest trips also have a tendency to take the most. Ethnic tourism, it seems, can become addictive (Riley 1988).

An extreme example of "travel addiction" is provided by a young couple from Amsterdam met at the Cañon del Sumidero. He, a bank employee, and she, a secretary, began saving for a two-year trip around the world in 1986. They started traveling in August 1988, with a $35,000 budget ($25 a day per person), and had already been in Egypt, Kenya, Zambia, Zimbabwe, Malawi, Tanzania, India, Nepal, Thailand, Malaysia, Indonesia, the United States, and Mexico. Their style was to spend about two or three months in most of these countries, and their last stop on this trip was a three-month stay in Antigua, Guatemala, to learn Spanish. They got malaria in Africa and amoebic dysentery in Nepal, but this was hardly a deterrent to their wanderings, and they were only reluctantly contemplating a return to "normal" life. To them, *traveling* was life. Their style of travel has been reported in many parts of the world (Cohen 1982a; Riley 1988; Vogt 1976), and is sufficiently common to have spawned a multilingual literature of "alternative" travel guides.

We now have a statistical snapshot of what tourists who come to San Cristóbal are like. A few trends and types emerge from the numerical categories. Aggregate statistics, however, tend to hide more than they reveal, or to reveal merely the more obvious and the less interesting. In the next chapter, I shall try to convey the diversity of ethnic tourists rather than the uniformities. I shall endeavor to make the tourists come to life through vignettes.

TWENTY-FIVE VIGNETTES

6   THE TOURISTS

Perhaps the most interesting conclusion from the sample of
175 tourists is the extraordinary variety of their travel styles and motiva-
tions. This diversity can best be captured in twenty-five vignettes, se-
lected, to be sure, from among the more interesting interviews, and
some of them representative of several similar cases, but not exhaustive
of the variations. The sketches describe real individuals, not reconstructed composites, but all names have been altered to secure anonym-
ity. The twenty-five cases include eight U.S. citizens, five Germans, four
Frenchmen, two Mexicans, two Japanese, two Canadians (one Franco-
and one Anglo-Canadian), one Swede, and one French-speaking Swiss.
Eleven are men and fourteen are women, but in most cases travel com-

panions of the opposite sex are included in the sketches. Their ages range from fifteen to seventy-nine, with an average of thirty-nine. A more disparate collection of travelers would, I believe, be difficult to assemble in most tourist destinations.

1. Germaine, a Frenchwoman of sixty-four, and a retired shopkeeper from Lyon, is on her first trip to Mexico, an organized bus tour that rushes her in ten days from Mexico City to Cancún, for $170 a day, not including the airfare to and from Mexico. She travels with her husband, a Spanish civil war refugee, and a score of other Frenchmen from Lyon. She is a seasoned veteran of other organized tours to Saudi Arabia, Egypt, the USSR, Turkey, the French Caribbean, Greece, Thailand, and Burma. She is an enthusiastic buyer of artifacts, for which she bargains with gusto. When I interviewed her, she was carrying a plastic bag crammed with some $30 worth of belts, bracelets, cooking gloves, and other local textiles just purchased from Chamula women in the Santo Domingo market. Concerned that she might have been cheated, she showed me two silver bracelets purchased for $15 each in San Juan Teotíhuacan. They were so cheap, she told me, that she doubted they were made of silver, and she was pleasantly reassured when I authenti-cated the official Mexican "925" silver stamp. She bought so much, she told me, that she would not be able to close her suitcase. Her most vivid impressions were of the markets. She even bought a small sample of some twenty-five varieties of beans. "One does not see that anywhere else anymore," she told me, referring to the color and heterogeneity of the San Cristóbal markets. She and her husband liked Mexico a lot, but were extremely bitter and indignant at the humiliating treatment he had received at the hands of the U.S. immigration authorities during their transit through New York. As a Spaniard, it seems, he needed a U.S. transit visa, which he did not have, and he was kept under guard, separated from all others including his wife, and escorted to the plane by two immigration agents "as if I had been a drug trafficker." Never would he or his wife set foot in the United States again. In all their travels, it was the worst experience they had ever had.

2. Luís is a thirty-eight-year-old Mexican, of elite background, so Euro-pean looking that I first mistook him for an Argentine or a Chilean. A university graduate in public administration, he is a self-employed entrepreneur in construction. Until now, he has lived with his thirty-year-old German wife in Mexico City, but they are on their way to their new home in Cancún. He speaks fluent English, and is highly cosmopolitan, intelligent, articulate, and well-informed about world affairs. His wife, Lore, is fluently bilingual in German and Spanish. She came to Mexico as a ten-year-old girl with her German parents, who own a big pastry shop and a steel factory in Mexico City. She, too, is a university graduate, and indeed studied for a year in Stuttgart. Luís's hobby is colonial architecture, and he describes himself as a "lover of colonial art." He and Lore are frequent overseas travelers, and they travel independently. They know the Americas from Canada to Argentina, Europe, the Caribbean, North Africa, and the Middle East, and they intend to visit Guatemala on this trip before reaching Cancún. Luís and Lore are enchanted with the colonial character of San Cristóbal, and spent much time visiting the Cathedral, Santo Domingo, and other colonial churches and houses. In the Santo Dominto church, they sat for some twenty minutes, waiting for a mass to finish, so that they could freely circulate in the church and examine at leisure the famous carved wood pulpit, the gilded altarpieces, the paintings, and the side chapel. Well versed in styles and in the Catholic iconography, they exchanged informed, appreciative comments on the architectural richness of Santo Domingo. They are, in short, a simpatico, worldly, cosmopolitan, sophisticated couple, exploring the cultural richness of Mexico. Two of Luís's brothers are antique dealers, and he recalled with pleasure a buying trip on horseback taken many years ago in the remote hinterland of Oaxaca State. Luís is proud of his country, sensitive to its cultural richness, but at ease in North America and Europe. They stay at small, unpretentious two- or three-star hotels, and spend about $10 a day per person in San Cristóbal, which they described as very cheap (regalado) and marvelously quaint. They travel in their late-model VW Rabbit.

3. Kozo is a twenty-four-year-old Japanese who lives in Brazil, where he is an architecture student. He emigrated to Brazil as a ten-month-old infant, with his Japanese parents, and he still travels on a Japanese passport, although he now describes himself as culturally more Bra-

zilian than Japanese. Besides Japanese and Portuguese, he also speaks fairly fluent Spanish and English. He is in the middle of a long, slow trip, mostly by bus, from Brazil to Toronto, via Belice, Guatemala, Mexico, and the United States. Last year, he was in Cuba and Canada. He travels alone, stays in cheap posadas, eats on the streets and in markets, and spends between $10 and $15 a day, including transportation. He bought some $6 worth of textiles in the Santo Domingo market to bring back as small gifts to his family, but does not purchase much because he travels light, out of his backpack. Extremely articulate, he is interested in anthropology, especially in problems of development and westernization. He likes San Cristóbal because it is a tranquil, undeveloped colonial town with a strong Maya tradition. On the other hand, he hates Cancún, which to him epitomizes the destruction of nature for the sake of a kind of tourism he abhors. Cancún represents to him the American way of life. But Europeans, he notices, prefer to come to the more interesting parts of Mexico. Kozo is especially irritated when he sees signs in Japanese, because to him that represents the ultimate in capitalist penetration, the very thing he seeks to escape in his travels.

4. Hildegard is a forty-five-year-old medical assistant from Germany on her second trip to Mexico, where she will spend thirty-five days with her German companion, Hermann, an academic and cell biologist who has been in Mexico five times, and combines his tourism with the collection of fish specimens for his research. They travel in a rental car, spend about $65 per day per person, stay in good hotels, and like to travel comfortably though not luxuriously. They are interested in colonial architecture and were attracted to San Cristóbal because the Santo Domingo church facade was on the cover of their guidebook. Their tour also took them to most of the Maya ruins of Yucatán and Chiapas, as archaeology is also one of their main interests in Mexico. They speak enough Spanish to get by, but are not fluent in it. They used to like Puerto Escondido, but find it too developed now, almost another Acapulco. At the Santo Domingo market they bought two little dolls from a Chamula woman during our interview, more to be rid of her and do her a favor than because they wanted them. They did not ask the price, much less bargain. Hermann gave the woman a 10,000 peso note (about $3.50). The woman looked at him, trying to assess how much change to give back, and correctly judged that she could grossly short-change him without eliciting protest. The 3,000 or 4,000 pesos he received in change were immediately distributed among half a dozen Chamula children who had gathered around and started begging, sensing Hermann to be a sympathetic and promising prospect for a donation. As more children quickly congregated around us, Hermann emptied his pockets of his remaining change, remarking that Mexican coins were so heavy and nearly valueless that they were not worth carrying in his pockets. Both he and Hildegard are very fond of Mexico and behave generously, as they have a feeling of guilt about their affluence in a poor country.

5. *Karl*, a thirty-two-year-old German car locksmith, is on a yearlong, 50,000-kilometer North American journey with his wife, a dressmaker, and their six-year-old son. The trio travels by Yamaha motorcycle with sidecar, on a budget of $8 a day per person. They started planning and saving eighteen months ago for the trip through the United States, Mexico, and Guatemala. This traveling is "nature-oriented, not city-oriented"; they camp in national parks if possible, and they cook their own food on a gas stove. They have a total budget of 23,000 DM ($15,000) for the three of them for the year. His wife gave up her job, but Karl expects to get his old job back when he returns to Germany. They generally avoid big cities, but they like San Cristóbal because it is fairly small, though they seem to have little interest in either the town or its people. They come into town mostly to shop for food and wash their laundry. They speak almost no Spanish, and did not follow up on their idea of spending a couple of weeks in Antigua Guatemala to learn Spanish. They visited a few tourist sites, notably the pyramids of Teotíhuacan, but they are more interested in scenery and outdoor activities. Indeed, they climbed the Popocatepetl. They are critical of Mexicans for lacking environmental concerns, for littering along highways, and for what they see as neglecting the national parks. Altogether, they spent some 100 days in Mexico.

6. *Pierre* is a thirty-two-year-old Franco-Canadian who is on his third trip to Mexico. He travels with his Californian girlfriend, recently met in Tulum, in a rented Volkswagen, and spends about $40 per person per

day, including car rental. He is a freelance television producer and his trip to San Cristóbal is in connection with research for a six-hour TV series on Incas, Aztecs, and Mayas for the 500th anniversary of Columbus's "discovery" of the Americas. The series was four years in the making and will cost an estimated $600,000, for which he raised the capital himself. Last year, he did a prize-winning thirty-minute documentary on the Inti-Raymi festival in Cuzco. He speaks "some Spanish," besides French and English. He bought about $75 worth of clothes in San Cristóbal, to replace those stolen from his car in San Cristóbal. Despite the theft, which he blames on his negligence, he likes the town for its Indian atmosphere, for its cleanliness, for its "European feel," and for its good hotels and restaurants. He plans to spend six days in San Cristóbal and already visited the ruins of Toniná, near Ocosingo, the caves, the Cañon del Sumidero, San Juan Chamula, Na Bolom, the markets, textile cooperatives, and the Santo Domingo church. San Cristóbal is his favorite town in Mexico. As I interviewed him, he was leaving for the carnival of Chamula, and seemed surprised and disappointed when I told him that photography was not allowed in Chamula during carnival.

7. *Marianne*, a twenty-six-year-old French salesclerk, is on her first Mexican trip, and will stay for forty-five days. She spends about $15 a day, speaks very little Spanish, stays in cheap posadas, and travels by bus with her French boyfriend, an instructor of scuba diving. She epitomizes the travel philosophy of the French *Guide du Routard:* she loves to travel cheaply in Third World countries, spending her hard-earned money slowly on long vacations of several months a year. Previous trips took her to Indonesia, the West Indies, and French Polynesia (where she lived for three years). The current tour will take three months and include California and Guatemala as well as a long Mexican itinerary. Marianne seems to show little interest in the tourist sites, in the culture, or in the people. Her main concern appears to be how cheaply one can live somewhere. She likes Guatemala "one hundred times better than Mexico," because it is cheaper, and she finds that Mexico has become too expensive because it has been spoiled by U.S. tourists, whom she detests wherever she finds them. She feels that Mexicans seek to exploit tourists, ask too high prices, and are less

friendly than Guatemalans. She does not think she will ever come back to Mexico. It has been irreversibly spoiled for backpack tourism. The Americans are to blame.

8. *Bob* is a forty-year-old American university administrator on his second Mexican trip. He travels with his wife by bus and train, and spends $17 a day per person. Both speak fluent Spanish, and they are spending sixty days in Mexico, fifteen of them in San Cristóbal. Bob lived in Bolivia for a year as a high school exchange student. He also spent a year in Madrid during his junior year in college and he has two university degrees, in international relations and Latin American studies. His first Mexican trip was in 1981. Bob and his wife like Mexico a lot, and are primarily interested in colonial architecture and Indian culture. They also like the climate of San Cristóbal. They are eager ethnic tourists. They had already visited several Indian villages (Chamula, Zinacantán, Tenejapa), seen Na Bolom and the INAH museum, cruised the markets, attended two masses (in different churches), talked to a lot of locals, and enthusiastically spent some $350 on a wide range of textiles and other handicrafts at the Santo Domingo market and in various shops. In fact, when I saw them, they had become *vendors* at the market, trying to unload some of their cooking utensils and clothes to make room in their suitcases for their local purchases. Bob was sitting behind his little display on the ground, between Chamula women, apparently finding no buyer. His fall-back plan was to barter his wares against yet more local items. Their travel style is frugal but comfortable, and they stay at "small family hotels." Bob's wife, a jolly, corpulent woman and witty *raconteuse*, treated me to an amusing, self-deprecating story of how they were robbed of their luggage in the Oaxaca train station. "I can see that Mexican watching that big, fat, white pigeon waiting to be plucked," she said of herself. But she was not going to let that one unhappy experience spoil the hundred good things that happened to them in Mexico.

9. *Joe*, his wife, and ten children are not in the sample of tourists, as they are resident gringos, but their story adds a dimension to San Cristóbal ethnic heterogeneity. I met them in the lobby of the cinema, waiting to see an Eddie Murphy comedy. They looked like a vignette out of Ap-

palachia, shabbily dressed and groomed, the mother breast-feeding her youngest child and the rest of the brood evenly spaced at one- or two-year intervals, with three teenagers at the upper end. Joe is an Oregon lumberjack in his early forties. He works overtime and saves as much money as possible, living in a trailer. When winter comes, the family piles into the trailer and pickup truck, migrates southward to Mexico, and lives there at subsistence level (on a budget of $2 a day per person) until their money runs out. Then they repeat the cycle. On this trip, they had been in Mexico for seventeen straight months, two of them in Tulum until the onset of the rainy season, and then in San Cristóbal, chosen for its cheapness, where they camp in the San Nicolás trailer park. The parents speak no Spanish, but the older children have learned some through contact with Mexican children. The children spent three months in a local school, but did not like it. Now they are being "home-schooled," probably a euphemism for an extended vacation, since the parents are not even high school graduates. The cinema outing was a splurge which they could afford only in Mexico, where the admission ticket is 90 cents. Now their savings were running out, and they were planning their return trip to Oregon in the spring, when the melting snow would permit the resumption of logging operations.

10. Arthur, a forty-year-old American carpenter on his second trip to Mexico, is camping in his Dodge van, in the San Nicolás trailer park, where he will stay a month. He, too, is from Oregon, and likes to avoid the damp, chilly winters there. He describes himself as a "budget traveler" and "a lousy tourist," spending about $10 a day. His brother and his sister-in-law accompany him, and he is divorced. San Cristóbal was recommended to him by an American friend on the "gringo trail." He likes the town because it is "not Mexican, more like Guatemala, un-westernized." He describes his main activity as "driving around," and also has Guatemala and Belice on his itinerary. Critical of Mexico for the "attitude of *mordida,* dirt, and lack of environmental concern," he is, however, full of praise for one Mexican commodity: good, cheap liquor at $4 a liter. His principal activity when not on the road is to sip one drink after another in the shade of his van. "Laid-back," and with an excellent sense of humor, he seems to come to Mexico mostly because it is a cheap, pleasantly warm place to enjoy life and get away from what he dislikes most: work. He is not a "hippie," however. Indeed, his style of dress, his manners, his speech, and his politics are very "straight" and conventional. He might best be described as burned-out working class.

11. Denise, a twenty-six-year-old French-speaking Swiss, who has lived in Mexico for four years, and in San Cristóbal for a little over a year, is another denizen of the San Nicolás trailer park (fig. 38). She, her Mexican husband, Adolfo, and their two young children—a breast-fed infant and a toddler—live in a small shack, twelve square meters in size, with a dirt floor, and neither electricity nor indoor water. (They do, however, have access to the communal washroom of the trailer park.) Their budget is about $2 a day per person, and their living standard can best be described as bare subsistence, even by Mexican peasant standards, but clearly by choice, not by necessity. Denise seems to come from a bourgeois family, is highly educated and articulate, and calls herself a "jewelry craftsman," a part-time occupation she shares with Adolfo, who markets their production to tourists in town. She gave birth to their second baby in their shack with the assistance of a local midwife. An old, one-speed bicycle is their main means of transport, used in commuting from the trailer camp to the Santo Domingo market, where Adolfo sells their costume jewelry, and to La Familia, the counterculture restaurant where San Cristóbal's long-haired gringos hang out, and where they spend many relaxed hours in the company of artists, musicians, and sundry dropouts from the First World rat race. Her main complaints, shared by her husband, are police interference with their hawking, and attempts to extort bribes. She bitterly related the extortion of a $100 fine at the border, under threat of imprisonment, and without being given a receipt, for overstaying the date on her Mexican tourist card.

12. Judy is at the other end of the social spectrum. A seventy-nine-year-old American "homemaker" from Washington State, she is traveling with her eighty-six-year-old husband, Richard, a retired paper mill owner. I met them in the elegant restaurant, La Galería, where they were enjoying a good lunch. They are staying in the Diego de Mazariegos Hotel for ten days, out of a Mexican trip of a month's duration, their sixth visit to the country. Their daily budget is about $75 per person. Four of their prior trips were taken in their private plane (they each have a pilot's license), in the late 1940s and 1950s. When they became "too old to fly," they turned to sailing, and took several Mediterranean and Caribbean trips in their sailboat. Now, they are too old to sail, but they continue to be enthusiastic travelers. Their recent trips included South Africa, Afghanistan, Papua New Guinea, Cambodia, and Chile. They also like to visit an American friend who owns a 100,000 hectare cattle ranch in Durango. During their stay in San Cristóbal, they had visited by chauffeured rented car Chamula, Zinacantán, Palenque, and Agua Azul. They love San Cristóbal's climate, which seems to agree with Richard's asthma. San Cristóbal to them is the "real Mexico, away from the big cities," but they found the market already too urbanized for their taste. Mexico City they describe as "a madhouse," and they yearn for the peace and quiet of small towns and open country. They love Mexico and seem to treat lightly a recent bad experience when Richard had his wallet pinched by two children working as a team in the Oaxaca Zócalo. They are experienced enough travelers, however, to have carried not much of value in the wallet. Judy speaks fluent French (she once lived in France for a year) and some Spanish. Both she and Richard are highly educated, sensitive, articulate people, although Richard's hardness of hearing cut him off from much of the interview.

13. Irmgard is a fifty-two-year-old German secretary on her first trip to Mexico. She spends $15 a day, travels alone by bus, and intends to spend twenty-one days in Mexico. She likes to take a long trip every year, always independently, and she particularly likes Brazil, where she has been often. She speaks some Portuguese and Spanish. When interviewed, she had already seen the two markets and the INAH museum, and she had walked around town. She found the natives friendly and helpful, and the town so clean that she felt guilty about spitting out the seeds of the tangerines she had just bought at the market. She seemed at ease with the Chamula women in the Santo Domingo market, though somewhat guilty about their poverty. For example, she first bargained for three belts (normally selling for 3,000 pesos each) from 15,000 pesos to 13,000, and then ended up paying 15,000 anyway because the woman seemed to need the money. Irmgard then took the woman's photograph, and the Chamula obligingly and spontaneously pulled off her sweater to look more Indian in her traditional blouse. Irmgard also asked another Chamula to pose for her, but she refused unless Irmgard bought something from her. Irmgard also felt sorry for the Indian children who all seemed to have snotty noses and colds. In short, Irmgard seems a typical, considerate ethnic tourist with a mild liberal guilt complex, but nonetheless able to enjoy cultural diversity and to adapt well to the host country.

14. Marc, a twenty-six-year-old Canadian from Vancouver, is a prototypical "hippie," describing his profession as "pilgrim." His striking appearance made him extremely conspicuous for the few hours he was around the Santo Domingo market and the La Familia restaurant. He walks around barefoot, with a long shepherd's crook, dressed in a striking wardrobe assembled at half a dozen Guatemalan Indian markets and including multicolored pants, shirt, belt, bracelets, several strands of bead necklaces, and a felt hat. His shoulder-length hair is appropriately disheveled, and his thick myopic eyeglasses are in the old-fashioned, rimless style. Marc spends some $7 a day, and travels with three friends met on the road, two Australians and a Mexican. He intends to spend four months in Mexico, Guatemala, and the United States, hitchhiking, walking, and taking buses. The *Lonely Planet* is his guidebook. He finds San Cristóbal very beautiful and came "to observe," though he was quite inarticulate when asked to specify *what* he wanted to observe. Indians, he thought, were simple people, living day by day, without a worry in the world, although he added in an afterthought of self-insight that perhaps he did not have enough time to find out what they really thought. At the Santo Domingo market, he was strongly attracted by a very worn embroidered vest of pseudotraditional style, and started bargaining energetically with the Chamula vendor in a voluble but largely unintelligible verbiage consisting mostly of English words with Spanish-sounding vowel endings. The vendor wanted 25,000 pesos; he offered 15,000; she went down to 18,000 and he finally walked away without buying, but only after a long bargaining session which he seemed to enjoy for its own sake. Two hours later, he was sitting on the steps of the Caridad church, bedecked in a just-acquired

Zinacanteco poncho, and surrounded by a circle of Chamula children. This time, he was trying to buy a scarf from the back of a Zinacanteco man who wanted twice the going rate. He then returned to the Chamula woman with whom he had bargained for the vest, and ended up paying 20,000 pesos for what he had previously bargained down to 18,000. Another half hour later, he had bought a white Chamula poncho, and ended up in La Familia, where his kaleidoscopic appearance was striking even in that colorful counterculture crowd. He shared a posada room with his three travel companions for 4,000 pesos each (about $1.75).

15. Gisela, a thirty-year-old German nurse, fits the profile of the politically conscious tourist with a heavy liberal guilt syndrome. She is traveling with another German woman of approximately the same age and political orientation. Together they will spend four months in Mexico and twenty-one days in San Cristóbal, traveling by bus, on a daily budget of $11. They will also visit Guatemala and the United States. She speaks some Spanish, read about Mexico before leaving Germany, and visits the usual tourist sights, including Chamula, Zinacantán, the church of Guadalupe, and Na Bolom. She finds San Cristóbal a nice little town with very friendly people in spite of much tourism. However, she is uncomfortable being "a rich tourist surrounded by poor Indians," saddened when approached by Indian vendors in restaurants, and shocked to see children working late at night. Exploitation of people in the Third World troubles her and spoils her pleasure in traveling.

16. Pablo, a fifty-five-year-old Mexican lawyer from a nearby town, frequently visits San Cristóbal with his wife and two children. San Cristóbal is his favorite town in Chiapas, because of its people, its culture, its churches, but mostly because of its cool, high altitude climate. He comes on weekends to escape the heat of the low country where he lives (Ocosingo), stays in a good hotel, travels in his own car, and spends about $20 per day per person. Pablo has both friends and relatives who live in San Cristóbal, and "never tires of it." On this trip, he bought textiles in the Santo Domingo market for about $80. Unlike most foreign tourists, but like most local Mexicans, Pablo finds that San

Cristóbal improves from year to year with the development of tourism. Tourism is a great thing. It brings in money. New restaurants and hotels are springing up all the time. The town modernizes, develops, becomes cleaner. What could be better for San Cristóbal? He only wishes that the trees growing on the *cerro* near the Zócalo could be cut down, because they are beginning to block the view of the town. And the television reception in the hotel rooms should be improved by the installation of satellite antennae.

17. Jan, a fifteen-year-old American, travels with his Dutch mother and his baby brother. All go barefoot, dress in drab, loose-fitting robes, and live on "almost nothing"; 50,000 pesos (about $18) easily last the three of them for a week. They travel by bus, and they come from the United States and Canada, where they live "in the National Forest" during the summer months. They migrate down to Mexico and Guatemala when the weather gets too cold for outdoor living in the north. Jan and his mother (who breast-fed the baby twice during our forty-five-minute interview) are concerned that the baby should commune with Mother Earth by crawling naked on it. They have spent some two months in Mexico this year, and have no fixed travel plans at all. At first they found Mexico very dirty, but now they realize that it is simply different from the rest of North America, with greater population density. They are heavily into organic food, and they currently live in a nearby commune made up of Mexican Indians, Germans, Frenchmen, and others who are running an organic farm. They help with the work, and they share the food. They eat rice, beans, tortillas, fruits, and vegetables. Jan's mother studied at Utrecht and Leiden universities and was a teacher, but she "dropped out." Both Jan and she are fluently bilingual in English and Dutch, and speak some Spanish as well. They are intelligent and articulate. During the interview, the blond baby girl circulated among several admiring Chamula women who petted her on the head (blond hair fetishism is widespread among both Indians and ladinos in Chiapas).

18. Catherine, a French "retired mother" at age sixty-two, is on her first Mexican trip. She and her husband came from France to visit her brother, who married a Mexican and who is a hotelkeeper in Oaxaca. The four of them are taking a forty-five-day tour of the country in Catherine's brother's car. When asked how much they spent, Catherine replied with the French proverb: *Quand on aime, on ne compte pas* ("When one loves, one does not calculate"). They stay at the Diego de Mazariegos Hotel, which they find enchanting, and they did not even ask the price of the rooms. In fact, they never ask about prices, because everything is so cheap that they feel ashamed to bargain. Both Catherine and her husband are enthusiastic about the natural beauty of Mexico, with landscapes on a scale unthinkable in Europe. They are also charmed by the colorful Indian markets, the baroque churches, and the Indian villages. Catherine found her experience in Chamula especially moving. They were praying in the church, and an old man came to touch the head of her sister-in-law to bless her. Their travel style is highly organized. The itinerary was planned, and hotel reservations made by a Mexican travel agency, even though her brother is a long-term Mexican resident and in the hospitality business. They also follow the *Guide Bleu*, which they find very good for history, culture, and sites, but miserably inaccurate about restaurants and hotels. For example, the previous evening they had a poor meal in a recommended restaurant. However, Catherine finds Mexico a "discovery" far exceeding her expectations.

19. Karen, an American painter of thirty-four, has been in Mexico seven times, and in San Cristóbal four times in two years. On this trip, she will spend four months in Mexico and twenty-five days in San Cristóbal. She travels by bus with her Mexican lover, Jaime, on a budget of $20 a day per person. They are continuing on to Guatemala and Belice. Karen came to San Cristóbal to visit the Indian communities, and to find a tranquil place to paint. She also likes to wander in the countryside. Even though there is a lot of tourism in San Cristóbal, tourism is not oppressive as in the Caribbean. It is low-keyed and much less expensive than on the coast. You can still talk to people here. (She is fluent in Spanish.) On the coast the horrible hotel architecture is destroying nature. She is afraid that San Cristóbal, too, is going to change for the worse. At this point in the interview, Jaime interjected and launched into a virulent political statement. An angry, radical, long-haired young man of about twenty-five, he bitterly complained about the destruction of the environment by tourism, the alienation of Mexicans from their own towns in the tourist resorts, the horrible architecture of the hotels, and the policies of the Mexican government toward tourism "development." "Tourism is fucking up everything, you understand?" (*El turismo está chingando todo ¿me entiendes?*) "I was lucky not to have been born a terrorist." He would like to throw bombs all over Cancún and destroy the whole place. Jaime also exploded with rage over the racial discrimination he experienced in the United States. "Those fucking yankees treat us like dirt in the United States, yet we Mexicans treat tourists very well." Karen nodded in approval during the entire ten-minute monologue. (Jaime addressed me in the familiar "tu" form, in good radical rhetoric, but in violation of the age-deference etiquette, since I was at least thirty years his senior. Nevertheless, he was very friendly toward me despite his anger.)

20. *Michi*, twenty-two, is a Japanese student of Spanish at a Japanese university and travels with a female classmate. Besides her fluent Spanish, she also speaks some English, as does her friend. She has been in Mexico three times and in San Cristóbal twice. She travels by bus, spends some $15 a day, and is a classical backpack tourist: well-informed, inquisitive, alert, adventuresome, adaptable, and prepared to put up with discomfort to see remote places. On this trip, she is also visiting Guatemala, the United States, and Canada. She lived for a year in Buenos Aires, where her father taught English to Japanese students. It was that stay in Argentina that got her interested in Latin America. She decided to study Spanish at university, and now plans to apply her specialized knowledge to a career in the tourist industry. Interested in Maya civilization and Chamula religious beliefs, she visited Chamula (where she found the church "mysterious"), Zinacantán, and even remote San Andrés, by rickety, second-class bus. She often eats in market stalls, and camps in isolated villages. Although she found Guatemalan Indians more open and communicative than the Mexican ones, she enjoys San Cristóbal's quietness, pure air, colonial atmosphere, and Indian markets. She expressed amusement that in Guatemala she was

frequently mistaken for a Chinese, while in Mexico she was recognized as Japanese. She wondered why there was a difference between the two countries in the way she was perceived.

21. *Inge* is a thirty-one-year-old Swedish student of English literature who also worked in hotels, in a bank, in a theater agency, and as a stewardess on cruise ships. She speaks very little Spanish, and is in Mexico for the first time, but she is an experienced traveler. Previous trips took her to India, Nepal, Fiji, New Zealand, Australia, Singapore, and most of Europe. Her English is flawless, and she is extremely articulate. She travels alone, by bus, on some $20 a day, and this trip will also take her to Guatemala. She is an acute, perceptive, critical observer of the tourist scene. She finds San Cristóbal touristy, and remarked on the "cutesyness" of La Galería, but still, San Cristóbal "looks much more like my image of Mexico than Yucatán." She liked Palenque and the Indians of the highlands, but she is "freezing to death" in San Cristóbal and is leaving faster than she expected because the climate does not agree with her. In all, she will spend thirty days in Mexico and seven in San Cristóbal. On the whole, she is "not pleasantly surprised" by Mexico. She finds the poverty horrifying and the Mexicans "tired and lacking zip." Most shocking was to observe the behavior of tourists in Chamula. A tour guide took a group of tourists with huge cameras to invade people's privacy. A Frenchman even took his video camera inside a house. Tourists treat people as if they were in a zoo. Yet, San Cristóbal tourism is better than in Cancún, where tourists are interested only in the sand, not in Mexicans. Sexual harassment is also a constant concern for Inge in Mexico. A chap followed her in Palenque, and in Campeche she was really scared. She heard of a woman being assaulted in Agua Azul, but she feels safe in San Cristóbal.

22. *Anna* is taking her first trip to Mexico, Guatemala, and indeed, the Third World, in the company of fifteen other young Germans. She is twenty-three years old, and a surveying technician. The tour will last twenty-one days, by regular bus, and is privately organized by a Protestant pastor for young members of his Freudenstadt congregation. It is low budget. They share rooms in cheap hotels, and eat on the street.

Anna spends some $12 a day. She buys few artifacts because "you can't carry the stuff around." What little she bought, she acquired in Guatemala, which she finds more colorful than Mexico. But San Cristóbal is a clean, lively, pleasant town, much better than Cancún, which is not the "real Mexico." Anna speaks some Spanish, and the pastor who organized the itinerary lived many years in Mexico and is fluent in Spanish. All tour members see themselves as backpack tourists on a study trip, and are serious about getting to know Mexican people and culture.

23. *Andrew*, seventy-five, is a retired American journalist, former editor of the *Hungry Horse News*, and Montana's sole recipient of a Pulitzer Prize. Outwardly, he looks like a typical American tourist with his video camera and "middle-American" look, but he is, in fact, a critical observer and experienced traveler. (We met in the bank as I helped him pick up a wad of dollar bills he had let fall while exchanging $50 into pesos.) This is his eighth Mexican trip. With his wife and twenty-eight other Americans, he is part of an exchange group organized by the Friendship Force, an idealistic but nonsectarian outfit dedicated to the promotion of international peace through personal contacts. ("A world of friends is a world of peace.") Andrew and his wife will be hosted by a San Cristóbal family for the twenty days of their Mexican stay, and he, in turn, has hosted Brazilians and New Zealanders in years past. Group participants tend to be retired, middle-class people, mostly professionals, farmers, and businessmen. Andrew is loquacious and has definite opinions on many topics. He has liberal views on U.S. foreign policy and is extremely critical of U.S. intervention in Latin America. He feels Mexico needs economic help, but bemoans the fact that the aid gets only to the upper two percent of the population. Andrew likes Mexicans, whom he finds extremely friendly and hospitable, but he is critical of the "mañana philosophy," the inefficiency of small businesses, lack of punctuality, the population explosion, poverty, and pollution in the large cities. Andrew speaks some Spanish. He likes Pátzcuaro, Morelia, San Cristóbal, and Guanajuato but finds Acapulco and the other resort towns unattractive. He did some sightseeing in San Cristóbal, videotaping as he went along, but he did not accompany the group to Chamula and Zinacantán because he heard you could

not photograph there, and besides he had "seen enough Indians in Montana."

24. Angela, fifty-two, an American from Michigan, retired early from business office work. She is on her first Mexican trip, a 120-day journey with her husband, a retired mathematics and physics teacher, in their pickup and trailer. They stay in the more expensive Bonampak trailer park, which hosts a more middle-class clientele, compared to the downscale San Nicolás park. They love Mexico, are having a wonderful time, and feel safer from theft than they do in the United States. They especially like San Cristóbal for the climate and mountain scenery, but also because, unlike Tijuana and Veracruz, it is not a "tourist trap town." They were surprised to see how backward rural Mexico still was, with oxen plowing fields and people carrying wood on their backs. They had never seen that before. Mexicans, they think, are very helpful. People not only helped them when they had mechanical trouble on the road but insisted on giving them a straw hat (they were hat salesmen). Angela and her husband love to bargain. In fact, they believe it is expected of them. "Merchants like that. You know that they have goods overpriced." They heard that Japan had bought out Pemex for $35 billion. "Was that true?" they asked hopefully. In fact, Pemex is what they dislike most in Mexico. They found the service at the gas stations poor, and they were cheated in Veracruz when the pump was not set back at zero. Otherwise, they have no complaints. Tomorrow they plan a trip to Chamula and Zinacantán.

25. Marie-Claire, twenty-four, is a French student of English on her first trip to Mexico. She travels with her aunt and forty-three other Frenchmen on a ten-day organized bus tour. Her employer had given her a tour ticket for "services rendered"; otherwise she always travels independently. In recent years, she was in Thailand, Morocco, Tunisia, and the United States. She appears to have almost no interest in Mexican culture and is extremely critical of the tour. "One does not see what one would like to see. The bus trips are too long. Everything is done in a hurry. One only sees the touristy spots. I would have liked to have spent more time in Acapulco and the Pacific Coast. There was too much archaeology. This was a stone circuit." In short, she took the wrong tour, and is the antithesis of the ethnic tourist. She detests Mexico City, which she described as "dirty, noisy, dusty and disgusting, except for the anthropology museum." She is also eloquently disgusted about "smells of putrefaction in the markets. We quickly backtracked." In San Cristóbal, she bought leather boots and some silver jewelry for $90. She went to Chamula with Sergio Castro but did not go to his evening show at his home, and she estimates that two-thirds of the tour members stayed at the hotel as she did.

SUMMING UP

As these vignettes illustrate, even a small sample of tourists exhibits an astonishing range of characteristics and extremes. The parsimonious survive on $2 a day while the profligate spend $200. Those in a hurry "see" the town in two hours while the leisurely stay for months. The Philistines are totally unconcerned and ignorant about local culture and history, while the erudite prepare their trips months in advance through extensive reading. Some do not make the slightest attempt to communicate in Spanish while others take weeks of their trip to attend language schools. The sensitive and discreet express concern for poverty, disease, and invasion of privacy, while the callous treat locals as providers of services and amusements. To some, the town is a live society they seek to understand. To others, the town is a theater decor and the inhabitants a cast of colorful actors in a vast "natural" performance. Local textiles can be seen as the dress style of flesh and blood people, as disembodied art objects to be displayed in one's living room, or simply as trophies of conspicuous consumption in the chase of the exotic. The cultural relativist adjusts to the unusual and seeks explanations for what is disturbing, while the ethnocentrist condemns, criticizes, and expects his tastes to be catered to.

While some consider San Cristóbal quaint, pristine, and authentic, others regard it as touristy, artificial, and spoiled, and still others as backward and in need of further development. Some seek a pleasant climate, a clean, safe environment, good food, and comfortable hotels. Others are prepared to put up with physical discomfort and risks in their quest for the authentic, the exotic, and the unusual. The level of activity ranges from the sedentary café lounger content to watch the world go past, to the spastic camera bug stalking his prey. Anxiety levels about hygiene go from the unconcerned who "goes native" and buys food, cooked or raw, at the local market, to the hypochondriac who travels with a portable pharmacy, selecting the day's nutrients with the fastidiousness of a dietician. (The menu of La Galería, for instance, reassures its clients in four languages that all salads have been thoroughly disinfected.)

Some tourists come to San Cristóbal by accident, have never heard of it before, mispronounce its name, and generally travel in an almost totally unplanned, unscheduled, and unprepared manner, wandering from town to town by the blind draw of the bus schedule, and, I suspect, without any clear geographical notion of where they are. At the opposite extreme, others leave nothing to chance, follow a fine-tuned itinerary, reserve their hotel rooms weeks in advance, follow walks recommended by their guidebook (held open with a finger at the relevant page), and carry in their head a mental map of all their movements. A number of tourists, for example, carried around three or four guidebooks in two different languages, and complained about the unavailability of good, detailed regional maps in the local bookstore.

Degree of independence of travel also ranges widely. Some tolerate only solitary travel while others contentedly let themselves be herded by their tour guide, are anxious about losing their way, and panic when out of sight of their group. The American outfit, Caravanas, for instance, which organizes trailer convoys, dresses up its participants in blue windjackets and baseball caps so they do not lose sight of each other in crowded Mexican streets or markets. (It also makes them prime targets for pickpockets, as they tend to be naive and inexperienced travelers.) Unhappiest of all are the semi-independent, not quite trusting themselves on their own, who belatedly find themselves captive in a group not to their liking and who mourn their temporary loss of freedom.

Clearly, all this diversity is not easily reducible to a typology. There are certain nationality stereotypes commonly held by both tourists and locals. North Americans, for instance, are the butt of everyone else's ridicule as naive, uncultured tourists who congregate in the resorts and are easy marks for exploitation. One American, aware of that stereotype, even answered "American, I am ashamed to confess," when I asked him his nationality. Enough fit the stereotype so comically well as to reinforce it, yet our vignettes show that many do not, while many non-Americans do. Japanese have the reputation of being gregarious tourists and undiscriminating buyers of artifacts at grossly inflated prices, yet the few Japanese who make it to San Cristóbal tend to be independent, adventuresome, well informed, and careful in their purchases. The French are often seen as stingy, suspicious, but knowledgeable tourists on the lookout for bargains, as some were, to be sure, but more were not.

Yet there *are* some modal differences between nationalities. Mexican tourists are quite different from foreign ones on a number of dimensions. They tend to be predominantly middle and upper class, because the Mexican working class (unlike its European counterpart) is still too poor to travel much for pleasure. Naturally, Mexicans tend to travel more in their own cars, to stay with friends and relatives, to seek relaxation and a change of climate rather than cultural exoticism, and, if they stay in hotels, to demand a quality of service they see as commensurate to their class status. Mexican tourists take their class status with them on their internal trips more than foreign tourists do in Mexico. (You have to know the Joneses before you have an incentive to keep up with them!) Hotelkeepers generally prefer foreign guests, whom they say tend to be less demanding and more honest (in such matters as stealing towels, as several hoteliers told me they were ashamed to admit). Also, Mexican hotel guests attach much importance to having television in their rooms, while foreign guests do not. In some smaller hotels, rooms with TV sets are, in effect, reserved for Mexicans, because foreigners seldom request or watch television in a language they do not understand.

Mexican and foreign tourist attitudes toward development, social conditions, and environmental issues also tend to diverge. Foreign tourists, especially ethnic tourists, want to see as little development as possible, and most enjoy a pristine, picture-book, colonial Mexico which most Mexicans regard as more backward than colorful. Many Mexicans, on the other hand, have a booster mentality which makes them look at modernity as progress, and mass tourism as a national asset. Mexicans are, as yet, less concerned about environmental degradation, or at least they are unwilling to sacrifice development to the altar of conservation. Foreigners, on the other hand, tend to be critical of pollution, littering, and other environmental insults, an attitude easy enough to understand. They want Third World countries to preserve clean, pristine playgrounds for them, without having to pay any cost, while happily continuing to contaminate their own polluted environment which their money allows them to escape. The Rhine can become an industrial sewer so long as you can take your vacation on a clean Amazon.

As for social conditions, Mexicans, especially the high status Mexicans who do most of the traveling, tend to take poverty, class differences, rural neglect, child labor, unemployment, shanty towns, and so on, for granted, because of constant exposure and familiarity with them. To many foreigners, especially those on their first Third World trip, these conditions are unfamiliar and shocking. Some, of course, expected to see them and succeed in not letting them spoil their vacation. Other seasoned travelers have seen much worse in Asia or Africa, and do not consider Mexico a really poor country. However, the "guilty liberal syndrome" of accepting a share of responsibility for social inequality and its consequences is exhibited by a certain number of sensitive ethnic tourists, who, at least in this study, tended to come mostly from Germany, the Netherlands, and Scandinavia.

In the end, however, individual variation overwhelms group trends and regularities. Probably more than other forms of tourism, ethnic tourism attracts a wide range of people for a great many different reasons. Many ethnic tourists are highly independent and individualistic, and seek in their travel a release from the constraints of their regular life. Their quest is not only for the other, but also for a release from themselves.

7 TOURISM AS ETHNIC RELATIONS

In the last analysis, tourism is a system of social relations, and more specifically of ethnic relations. Ethnic tourism brings together three groups with different cultures, class backgrounds, and interests: tourists who are attracted by the "otherness" of the natives, the natives who are the spectacle and whom I called tourees, and the middlemen who help bring the first two groups together and who largely benefit from this interaction. The complex system of interactions between all of these groups can be seen as a special form of ethnic relations, since these interactions clearly take place across ethnic lines. Even though each of these three groups may be further subdivided into several ethnic groups (as is true in San Cristóbal), each group finds itself in a sufficiently similar structural situation in the system of tourist interactions that it can be regarded as a kind of super-ethny.

THE BACKGROUND

In the preceding two chapters, we have seen who the tourists are. The tourees—those whom the tourists come to see—are the people North Americans rather inappropriately call "Indians," and the Mexicans more accurately call *indígenas*. It is the tourees' cultural and linguistic distinctiveness from the majority of the Mexican population that makes them attractive to ethnic tourists. They speak several Mayan languages, principally Tzotzil and Tzeltal near San Cristóbal, and are further subdivided into local communities, each with a distinctive style of dress, customs, political institutions, and so on.

A great debate over what Amerindians really are rages in the social science literature. Marxist intellectuals in Latin America tend to view them primarily as an oppressed Fourth World peasantry caught in an exploitative system of archaic and dependent capitalism which grew out of colonialism and now perpetuates itself on the periphery of the "world capitalist system." North American, "liberal" social scientists have tended to stress more their cultural and linguistic distinctiveness than their class position, and to look at Indian-mestizo relations more as ethnic than class relations. (See Colby and van den Berghe 1961; Stavenhagen 1964; Goldkind 1963; and Colby and van den Berghe 1964, 1965, for a version of this old debate in the local context of highland Chiapas.) The fact, of course, is that Mexican (and other) Indians are *both* culturally distinct, conquered nations that have been decapitated of their upper classes *and* the exploited peasantry of a modern class system.

In any case, the debate is of little consequence for ethnic tourism, except insofar as the ethnic tourist is interested in the "Indianness," not in the "peasantness," of Indians. Indians are interesting precisely because they are *not* like the garden-variety, "acculturated" Mexican *campesino*. Little does it matter that much of what is now considered "typical" Indian culture, such as dress styles or the *cargo* system, is, in fact, of fairly recent, colonial, rather than of pristine, pre-Colombian, origin. The romantic vision of Indians that the ethnic tourist seeks to capture is that of the "living Maya," as epitomized in the title of Morris's recent (1987) book. Trudy Blom was the first San Cristóbal resident to make a living selling pristine, "stone-age," "living Maya" to the adventure tourists of the 1940s and 1950s. The long-haired Lacandones in their loose nightgown style dress fitted perfectly the Rousseauan image of the Noble Savage.

Soon, ethnic tourism spread to the supposedly less "primitive" and "pure" groups of the highlands, helped along by the new artsy-craftsy fad for weaving and pottery, to which the jaded children of the middle class in the industrial countries were turning in droves. The backstrap loom and the potter's wheel became quite the rage, and what better way was there to return to one's folksy roots than to drink at the fountainhead of Amerindian culture? A decade after the flower children of the 1960s, the mystique of environmentalism and the romantic myth of the Indian as living in harmony and balance with nature also fed into the development of ethnic tourism. Starting in the 1960s, Indians became fashionable, especially the ones that continued to produce colorful, "authentic" crafts. Clearly, the inhabitants of highland Chiapas and of neighboring Guatemala fit the bill. San Cristóbal, the picture-book colonial town, was surrounded by postcard-perfect Indians. What a winning combination!

There remained only for the local ladino bourgeoisie to seize this new opportunity for small and medium scale entrepreneurship. They became the middlemen by developing the infrastructure necessary to make the ethnic tourist feel physically and psychologically comfortable. The Indians, who were unwittingly becoming tourees, had already been coming to town for generations, to buy and sell. The natural stage for the ethnic spectacle was already set, in the marketplace. All that remained was to expand the hotel and restaurant capacity, open the tour agencies, expand the bus services, and so on. The groundwork necessary to make the Indian villages accessible by road was even being provided free of charge, thanks to the efforts of the Instituto Nacional Indígenista, who were unwitting tourism developers.

Several features make interactions in ethnic tourism particularly interesting. First, these interactions are *transient*. Of the three casts of actors, one has rapid turnover; most tourists come and go in a few days. The situation does not change rapidly, for one batch of tourists looks much like another (despite the great internal heterogeneity of the group, as we have seen). The people, however, change rapidly. The tourist flow beats to the pulse of arriving and departing buses. Each fresh puff of diesel fumes disgorges a new batch and removes an old one.

Transience has consequences for interactions. As any student of reciprocity knows, human relationships are especially open to cheating if the probability of ever meeting again is low. This is clearly the case with tourism, and many tourists do indeed feel cheated and exploited. In fact, this is what people mean when they say that they are being treated as a tourist: their ignorance is being taken advantage of, they are being overcharged, promises are not fulfilled, and so on. Many tourists seek relationships with natives uncontaminated by greed, but find these all the more difficult to establish as tourism is more developed. Tourism, in short, breeds exploitation and abuse because bad behavior largely goes unpunished.

There are some correctives, of course, the main ones being word-of-mouth recommendation or warning, and guidebooks. Neither, however, is very effective, because of the time lag between bad behavior and its adverse consequences. By the time the new edition of the *Guide Bleu* or the *Lonely Planet* reports the salmonella epidemic in restaurant X or the bedbugs in hostel Y, the cook or the management has changed, and the wrong person gets punished while the culprit goes scot-free.

Second, interactions take place *across ethnic lines*, a condition which frequently makes for tension, mistrust, and misunderstanding. The language barrier is the most obvious source of lack of mutual understanding, but not the only one. Ethnocentrism also creates much tension. Tourists and natives constantly shock one another by behaving in unaccustomed ways and judging the others by their own standards. The consequences of such shocks can range from irritation to tragedy. A few examples will illustrate. Several young women complained to me of sexual harassment, probably not realizing that, within the context of Mexican culture, they were attired in a way which young Mexican men could only interpret as inviting, if not provocative. A young American naturopathic physician (and cleanliness freak) was horrified at the Mexican practice of throwing used toilet paper in a wastebasket next to the toilet rather than flushing it away. (The practice dates from the long-gone days of using newspaper, which clogged up toilets.) Mexicans, on the other hand, find scanty dress in churches or nudity on beaches offensive and disrespectful.

Photography is a frequent source of tension over invasion of privacy. A tragic episode involved the fatal stoning of a French tourist at the carnival of San Juan Chamula, a few years ago. He had been warned repeatedly not to take photographs and disregarded the warnings, not because he did not understand them, but because he misjudged their seriousness. No doubt, he was insensitive and deserves little sympathy, but this kind of breakdown of communication is especially likely to occur in interethnic situations. When guidebooks began to report his death as a warning to other tourists, however, some tourists overreacted, thinking the warning applied to the whole of San Cristóbal, and became quite diffident about taking pictures anywhere.

Third, ethnic tourism interactions involve highly *asymmetrical* relations. Tourists are rich and privileged compared to most natives, but relatively ignorant or naive about local conditions, prices, and so on. This unusual combination, of wealth and ignorance on one side, and poverty and knowledge on the other side, gives each party to the interaction advantages over the other. Each can easily resent the other and feel exploited, for different reasons and on different grounds. The tourist, for instance, feels cheated on the quality of a product or the price of an object, while the touree resents loss of privacy, perceived ridicule, or the economic necessity to sell at a low price. The variations are infinite but the potential for mutual hostility or ambivalence is enormous.

Given these tension-producing properties of transience, cross-ethnicity, and asymmetry inherent in ethnic tourism interactions, one might ask why they take place at all. The reason is not far to seek: the benefits of the interactions override the costs most of the time. Tourists may be envied, ridiculed, or resented, but they do bring in money. Conversely, tourists may feel cheated, short-changed, or ill-treated, but they still enjoy the spectacle enough to keep coming. Each tries to control the behavior of the other, and to seek or avoid situations or locations where the costs of interaction would outweigh the benefits. On both sides, interaction is thus a calculated risk, consciously manipulated to maximize satisfaction. In brief, tourists seek to avoid "touristy" situations—that is, situations in which they are treated as tourists. Tourees and middlemen endeavor to part the tourist from as much money as possible, without either chasing him away or seeing more of him than they want.

DAILY INTERACTIONS: GUIDED TOURS

The pattern of tourist interactions with either tourees or middlemen is largely determined by whether tourists are independent or come with guided tours, and by whether or not they speak Spanish. Guided tour members, nearly all Europeans, and disproportionately French, interact least with natives. On a typical tour, they arrive by bus late in the afternoon and are taken directly to their hotel, where reservations have been prearranged. The leader is usually an attractive, educated, young Mexican woman, often from Mexico City, who is fluent in the language of the tour. Almost all tours consist of people speaking the same language and nearly always of the same nationality. (I did, however, see a Belgian tour where some people spoke French and some Dutch.) The tour leader is in charge of all local arrangements, speaks to the hotel manager and personnel, and shepherds the group to the reception lobby while porters unload the luggage (mostly expensive matched-set suitcases), and escorts the guests to their respective rooms. The group generally dines in the hotel restaurant. After breakfast the next morning, the tour guide takes the group on foot to the produce market and walks them through in about fifteen minutes, returning by way of Santo Domingo to shop for handicrafts. In their absence, the tour bus will have been reloaded with baggage at the hotel (fig. 33), and the bus now awaits the group at the Zócalo.

Depending on how hurried the tour is, it may either leave around 10:00 a.m. for Palenque, Villahermosa, or some other destination, or take the group to San Juan Chamula for an hour's visit (figs. 14, 17, 18), followed in the afternoon by a visit to Na Bolom, more shopping, and, in the case of French tours, a slide show about Indians at Sergio Castro's museum. The less hurried tours will spend two nights in San Cristóbal and leave on the morning of the third day after breakfast at the hotel. Guided tour members talk mostly to each other. Most of their dealings with middlemen are filtered through the tour guide, who also delivers an abundant flow of information (not always very accurate or knowledgeable, since she is rarely a local) as she herds her flock from sight to sight.

"Free time" is limited to shopping and sometimes the midday meal, but even then opportunities for interaction are limited by both lack of time and ignorance of Spanish. Interactions with tourees are largely limited to turning down the solicitations of persistent Chamula vendors in the streets, or bargaining with them in the Santo Domingo market. Bargaining is usually short for lack of time, and inept for lack of knowledge of prices and local conditions. Tour members may occasionally talk briefly to a restaurant waiter or a ladino shopkeeper, but only as far as their Spanish allows, and for utilitarian purposes. Other than looking and buying, tour members sometimes do a little frantic church visiting, usually in Santo Domingo or La Caridad, where they spend between fifteen seconds and two minutes. The fifteen-second tour takes the form of a circular look from the entrance door; the two-minute tour is a quick walk down the central nave and back. Their shopping in the market is usually accompanied by rapid-fire photography, with a sexual division of labor: the husband takes pictures while the wife shops. Not uncommonly, the husband photographs his wife while she shops, poses her with the Chamula seller, or makes her model her latest purchases of hat or belt. The more sophisticated photographers try to take unposed pictures of Chamula women and children with a telephoto lens, but Indian women usually turn away their heads and call back their children, unless one buys from them first.

Locals often make fun of group tourists because of the way they move in unison, seem lost and bewildered, and display their ignorance of local conditions. Their often lavish, indiscriminating spending habits and their ineptness at bargaining make them favorites with merchants, both ladino and Indian. Chamula women are quick to take advantage of both their lack of Spanish and their ignorance of prices. Sometimes bargaining takes the form of reciprocal finger showing, but often items are bought without asking the price. The tourist then gives a banknote, say 10,000 pesos. The seller tries to ascertain whether the buyer expects change, and, if so, shortchanges the buyer as much as she dares.

As guided-tour buyers typically grossly overestimate prices, they end up paying about twice as much as other tourists. Not only do they not know prices, they also are under time pressure to keep up with their group, and thus cannot bargain at leisure, or leave and do comparison shopping. They also fear losing the only opportunity to buy something they want. They often buy large numbers of small gifts for friends and family members at home, and they are less constrained by the necessity of having to carry what they buy, since nearly all the baggage handling is done by hotel servants. Sometimes, as purchases accumulate in bulging plastic bags, the shopper buys a multicolored Guatemalan bag to accommodate her mounting acquisitions.

Hotelkeepers, too, love guided tours. For one thing, they come in big batches of between twenty-five and forty, and therefore boost occupancy rates. Their arrival is predictable, thus simplifying service. They eat most meals in the hotel restaurant, which would otherwise be nearly empty, as the less hurried, better-informed tourists quickly find out that most of the best restaurants are not connected with hotels. Guided tour guests seldom complain, or even talk to the manager. They are efficiently processed to their rooms and through their fixed menu meal. In short, tours are a hotelier's dream, and are therefore sharply competed for. They make the difference between a hotel's success or failure, but only a handful of the better three-star hotels are of sufficient quality for tours. The Diego de Mazariegos Hotel is in the best position to compete for tours because of its prime central location, its size, and its two beautiful colonial patios, but it has a reputation for poor service among its other customers. Nothing, it seems, spoils a hotel manager faster than reliance on tour clientele.

DAILY INTERACTIONS:
INDEPENDENT TOURISTS AND TOUREES

Independent tourists interact much more with natives, and in more varied ways, than guided tour groups. Many more of them speak some

Spanish; their pace of travel is more leisurely and more flexible; and they tend to be more daring, exploratory, and adventuresome. Some actively seek contact with locals, both ladinos and Indians, and many more regret that language barriers prevent more meaningful interactions. There is, however, a small group of highly sensitive ethnic tourists who exhibit considerable guilt at what they consider their voyeurism of Indians, and who refrain from going to the Indian villages or feel uncomfortable there, as if they were visitors to a human zoo. This liberal guilt attitude seems to be predominantly a North European phenomenon. Most people who expressed it were left-leaning young Germans, Scandinavians, or Dutch. Interestingly, that attitude is restricted to Indian watching. They do not feel that way towards ladinos, therefore suggesting that their curiosity as ethnic tourists is limited to the more exotic. They do not self-consciously watch ladinos as they do Indians, and feel quite at ease in ladino San Cristóbal.

Independent tourists not only stay in San Cristóbal one or two days longer on the average than those on guided tours, but they move at their own pace, undriven by any kind of schedule, or even a list of sights they *must* see. A few tourists methodically and conscientiously "do" the churches, museums, and monuments, guidebook in hand, but by far the greater number simply read their guidebook's description of the town, make a mental note of what they want to see, locate these places on the map, and then start walking around, soaking in the atmosphere, stopping to rest, meandering, and "stumbling" onto interesting sights. Most make no effort to identify by name a church or house they like. Some, however, use the comfort, quiet, and privacy of a church pew to peruse their guidebook at leisure, without being pestered by the solicitations of Chamula vendors, begging children, or shoeshine boys.

In the produce market, some tourists buy fruit as well as sightsee, and stop to chat briefly with sellers, asking for the price of food, or for the name of a fruit or vegetable they have not seen before, or for the use of a strange product (such as bags of pine needles, spread over the dirt floors and patios of houses on festive occasions to give a pleasant smell and keep down the dust). A few even dare to sit down at the food stalls and sample some of the local cooked food. However, the produce market attracts only a minority of the tourists, and then only briefly (ten to twenty minutes on the average). A number of tourists are repelled by its sights (such as animal heads in the butcher section) and smells and by their fear of the pickpockets who operate in its crowded alleyways.

The Santo Domingo artisanal market, on the other hand, is a favorite haunt of tourists. They feel safe and comfortable there, because, compared to the produce market, it is much less crowded, much cleaner, and free of strong odors. The market is shaded by large trees and surrounded by stone benches and low walls where one can relax and loiter. Besides, the Chamula women sellers and their playing toddlers provide free entertainment and ideal photo opportunities.

Only a minority of the tourists enter the churches, and then, with rare exceptions, only for two or three minutes. In several half-hour observation periods in the church of Santo Domingo (one of the richest sixteenth-century baroque edifices in southern Mexico, and certainly the most spectacular church in San Cristóbal), only an average of six to eight tourists entered and took more than a fifteen-second peep from the door. (The observation periods were between 11:00 and 12:00 a.m., at the peak activity of the market, when between fifty and eighty tourists would be present outside.) In the words of one young French couple coming out of church after a ninety-second visit, and reporting their experience to another couple: *C'est vieux, mais c'est joli. C'est tout doré* ("It's old, but pretty. It's covered in gold leaf").

A small minority of lovers of colonial art spend as much as fifteen or twenty minutes in Santo Domingo, and may even wait out the end of a mass to be able to wander around freely. (A quadrilingual sign in Spanish, English, French, and German reminds visitors that the church is a place of worship, not a museum, and most tourists refrain from sightseeing during religious services.) The observed record length of stay by tourists in a San Cristóbal church was held by an American couple who remained for fifty-seven minutes during a Chamula religious service in Tzotzil in La Caridad. They told me afterward that they wanted to experience "a Maya mass," as they were Roman Catholics. (The service was not a mass, but a lay-led prayer meeting with folk music. The American couple thought it was a Chamula reinterpretation of the mass and were very moved.) Apart from these exceptions, however, few tourists show much detailed interest in colonial architecture. They seem to share the "when-you-have-seen-one-you-have-seen-them-all" approach to Mexican churches, and they are content to soak in the atmosphere of the town by simply "walking around," a frequent self-description of their activities.

Interaction between tourists and tourees takes place almost exclusively in the Santo Domingo market and on the Zócalo, another tree-shaded park with convenient benches where tourists, ladinos, and occasionally Indians like to sit down, chat, and rest, especially in the late afternoon and early evening. Most contacts are in the context of a prospective or actual commercial transaction. Either tourists are solicited by beggars, children peddling chewing gum, shoeshine boys, and Chamula women and girls selling weavings, or tourists approach sedentary Chamula vendors in the market. Most tourists are annoyed by the street solicitation, and the ladino town authorities would like to stamp it out, but are powerless to do so. Street hawking and begging are irrepressible both because economic desperation drives many Chamulas to them (especially those who have been expelled from their communities for conversion to Protestantism), and because the tourist response makes them marginally profitable. Children have learned to elicit pity by begging or selling in a whining refrain of *comprame* and *regalame* ("buy from me" or "give me"), and little girls sometimes succeed in extracting little donations by being coquettishly cute.

Many tourists at first respond by distributing small coins to children or beggars, and buying gum or small weavings, such as bracelets, to be rid of the people, but the ploy backfires, especially with children, who are quick to congregate around the more generous and friendly. A number of tourists, however, chat with children, who quickly drop their whining voices and become quite friendly and smiling when a real conversation is initiated.

Adult Indians behave with much more restraint and dignity than their children. The Chamula women hawking in the streets simply block the way of tourists on the narrow sidewalks and hold up their merchandise, mostly belts and bracelets, some fifty centimeters in front of people's faces, with little verbal comment except a matter-of-fact injunction: *Comprame.* They observe the gaze of tourists, who in turn quickly learn to ignore them and avoid looking at either the vendors or their merchandise. At the slightest show of interest in the wares, the vendors separate the item looked at from the rest, and try to put it on or around their prospective customer, who then either disengages quickly and leaves or gets caught and generally ends up buying.

Recent arrivals make especially attractive targets to the hawkers, as they do not yet know the prices, have not yet become blasé and saturated by mountains of similar merchandise, and have not yet stocked up on presents and souvenirs. On the other hand, when they are loaded with backpacks, fresh from the bus station and before they have found a hotel room, tourists are not in a buying mood. Therefore, the most vulnerable time to catch them is when they first come out of their hotel after unloading their baggage. Most hawkers, therefore, hover around hotels, especially in Insurgentes and Guadalupe streets, or on the nearby Zócalo.

At the Santo Domingo market, interaction between tourists and Indians takes a more relaxed form. There, the tourists initiate the exchange, while the Chamula women squat on the ground behind their wares and wait for the customers to come and stop in front of them. There is a minimum of outward competition between sellers, and I have never observed any attempt to entice a potential customer away from a neighbor, nor even an endeavor to intercept tourists or interfere with their departure. The pattern is for the seller to look at approaching tourists and to remain quiet until they stop in front of her display. Then the seller makes an attempt to establish eye contact by asking in a normal voice, *Compra algo?* ("Do you want to buy something?"). She also carefully watches where the eyes of the prospective customer settle, and then lifts for better viewing the item that seems to interest them. This behavior may be repeated three or four times with different items without much talk on either side, until the tourist either moves on or is "hooked."

In the latter case, the seller frequently stands up and steps up her energy level. She may, for example, get the customer to model an article of clothing (fig. 17). This is also the point at which the tourist begins bargaining, in Spanish if possible, but otherwise in finger language. All the Chamula women are fairly fluent in simple conversational Spanish, but none have made the effort to learn even a few words of any other European language.

Indeed, even among ladinos dealing with tourists, relatively few speak languages other than Spanish, or try very hard to learn them. One young cart pusher in the produce market makes a comic show loudly shouting a French-pronounced *attention* to clear his way, but, as far as I know, his knowledge of French extends no further. The only outstanding exception I encountered was the owner of El Tuluk (an excellent little restaurant deservedly recommended by the *Guide du Routard*), whom I saw sitting at a back table with a Dutch dictionary and phrase book. He already spoke some French, English, and German, and was now working on his Dutch. Some hotel or restaurant owners and managers speak fairly fluent French or English, but more as the by-product of a good education or work experience in the United States than as a conscious effort to cater to tourists. Natives generally expect tourists in San Cristóbal to speak Spanish, and most of them do, at least to a limited extent. Even in the two local schools that prepare young men and women for hotel management and the tourist trade, relatively little stress is put on foreign languages, and few of the pupils are fluent in any. Indeed, except for two or three Mexicans married to resident gringos, I do not recall any local person ever addressing me in anything but Spanish during my entire stay in San Cristóbal. This is quite unlike the situation in coastal resorts, where the obvious foreigner is generally addressed in English. In San Cristóbal, I do not recall hearing a single "Hey, Mister."

Returning to bargaining, the behavior takes many forms. If the tourist obviously knows the price of an item, the seller quickly goes down to her minimum selling price without much resistance. Minimum prices are stated in round figures and are remarkably firm and uniform throughout the market. For example, I wanted to see whether any woman would sell me a 1,000 peso headband for 900, and none of the eight I approached would accept that offer. When the tourist's bargaining reveals an ignorance of prices, the seller reduces her asking price very slowly and reluctantly and gives in only when the customer is on the point of leaving, even though the offered price may be as much as twice the minimum price. Many small items, such as armbands, dolls, and so on, are sold at three to five times the minimum price (for example, a bracelet selling at six for 1,000 pesos often sells for 500 pesos), either because many tourists find these prices so trivial as not to be worth bargaining for or because they find them so low that they are ashamed or guilty to bargain with poor Indians. On several occasions, I watched guilt-syndrome tourists desultorily bargain down an item, and, having succeeded in doing so, pay the asking price in the end. An American woman, for instance, was asked 15,000 pesos for two belts worth 3,000 pesos each. She ineffectively bargained them down to 13,000 pesos and ended up paying 15,000 (two and a half times the minimum selling price).

Many of the tourists feel sorry for the Indians, and this tempers their bargaining behavior, though many also believe that the seller will feel disappointed if they do not bargain. So they bargain, but only halfheartedly, and they often rationalize their purchases as an act of charity. (*Il faut bien faire marcher le commerce*, "One must help commerce along," was a spontaneous comment of three French tourists.) Some tourists distribute sweets to the children or give away secondhand clothes after completing a purchase from a Chamula. Some also try to prolong the interaction by expressing an interest in the seller's children, by letting their children play with Indian children, by squatting next to the seller and admiring her merchandise (fig. 44), by closely watching her weave or braid, by asking questions about her family, and so on. Most of the sellers welcome a show of interest, so long as it does not interfere with other sales.

In the Indian villages, tourist-touree interaction is even more restricted than in San Cristóbal. For one thing, Indians in the villages speak less Spanish than the sellers in town. For another, Indian villages, except on Sundays and feast days, are fairly private places. People stay at home, are away at work, and generally keep their distance from tourists. The main exception is San Juan Chamula (twelve kilometers by paved road from San Cristóbal), which receives scores of foreign visitors daily (figs. 14, 17, 18). Some come in tour buses, others in the crowded microbuses that run back and forth to San Cristóbal, and others in private cars (fig. 15). The village has a tourist office with a full-time employee who sells 1,000 peso tickets for admission to the church (fig. 16), and there is a row of roofed stalls where women sell much the same wares as in San Cristóbal (including Guatemalan imports), at similar prices (fig. 17).

In recent years, San Juan Chamula has received so many visitors that the behavior of children has been profoundly modified. A group of twenty to thirty children loiter permanently around the municipal building, waiting to pounce on incoming buses and cars. They beg or try to sell little dolls or armbands in a loud chorus of whining voices; they aggressively stretch their begging hands through car windows; and they immobilize vehicles by surrounding them (fig. 15). Adults deplore this undignified behavior so much at odds with Chamula tradition, but are powerless to prevent it. They blame tourists for spoiling their children, but at the same time welcome a new source of income in their impoverished economy.

The situation in Zinacantán is quite different, even though the village is just as accessible from San Cristóbal as San Juan Chamula. The flow of tourists is perhaps only a fourth or a fifth of what it is in Chamula; there is no tourist office; a few women sell textiles, but on a smaller scale than in San Juan Chamula (as, indeed, very few Zinacantecas sell textiles in San Cristóbal); there are no whining children; no one begs; and everyone behaves with cool, distant dignity, largely ignoring the tourists and barely returning their greetings. The main difference is in tolerance of photography. In Chamula, picture taking is tolerated everywhere except inside the church and during carnival. In Zinacantán, prohibition of photography is strictly enforced everywhere, at the risk of being thrown in jail and having one's camera smashed. Consequently, far fewer tourists come, even though the village is at least as attractive as Chamula.

Other villages receive even fewer tourists. Tenejapa, for example, is twenty-eight kilometers (half of them unpaved and rather rough) away on a winding mountain road. *Colectivos* (public microbuses) are infrequent, and tour buses never visit Tenejapa. Perhaps eight or ten tourists come, mostly by private or rented car, on the two weekly market days (Thursday and Sunday). There is a small cooperative selling local weavings, but otherwise there is virtually no sign of tourist presence. The municipality attempts to impose a photography fee, but the amount is negotiable and enforcement is lax.

The ethnic tourist's quest for "living Mayas" is fairly quickly satisfied by a visit to Na Bolom, a textile cooperative or two, an hour or so of sightseeing and bargaining for handicrafts in the Santo Domingo market, a quick walk through the produce market, an hour's visit to San Juan Chamula, and a few souvenirs and a roll of slides to take home and relive the experience. If the look at Indians is superficial, the actual interaction is even more so, impeded as it is by the language barrier, by the Indians' relative aloofness, and, in some cases, by the tourists' guilty bashfulness at people watching.

DAILY INTERACTIONS: TOURISTS AND MIDDLEMEN

On the whole, tourists interact more with ladino middlemen than with the main object of their curiosity, the Indians. They *look* more at Indians, but they *talk* more to ladinos. There are three main reasons for this. First, Spanish is more of a common language between them, and, of course, the few Mexicans who speak other European languages are all ladinos. Second, tourists and middlemen not only share more of a common language, they are also closer in customs, tastes, values, experiences, education, and so on. They share, in short, the same "global village," unlike the Fourth World peoples who are still largely outside of it. Third, nearly all the services consumed by tourists during their stay in San Cristóbal are controlled and provided by the ladino middlemen: hotels, restaurants, motor transport, travel agencies, pharmacies, banks, and so on.

Tourists constantly have to talk to ladinos to buy bus tickets, order meals, reserve a room, ask for directions, get a remedy against diarrhea, request fresh towels, mail postcards, telephone, inquire why the hot water does not seem to flow or the toilet to flush, and countless other mundane problems. Middlemen, especially hotel employees and restaurant waiters, are also a constant source of information about the location of sights, the opening hours of banks, shops, and museums, the safety of the tap water, the quality of restaurants, and so on. Indeed, the free and gracious dispensation of accurate information at the hotel reception desk or the restaurant table is implicitly accepted by both tourists and middlemen as a self-evident part of the service, even though it is not explicitly the job of, say, a waiter to be knowledgeable about banking hours.

A small minority of the middlemen are, in fact, information specialists, notably the travel agents and the professional guides. The key skill they possess is greater fluency in the main European languages, at a minimum in English, but preferably in French and German as well. These information specialists often have more prolonged contact with tourists whom they accompany on tours, dispensing knowledge, answering questions, serving as interpreters or negotiators, and so on.

The three main settings for tourist-middlemen interactions are hotels, restaurants, and shops. Tourists choose hotels primarily from the recommendations of guidebooks or other tourists, or through personal inspection. Many of the backpack tourists simply walk off the bus and start walking along Insurgentes, toward the center of town. Some, usually those who do not intend to stay long, stay at the Capri, near the bus station, but most seek a more central location near the Zócalo, where most hotels are situated. The younger backpackers generally opt for cheaper hotels or posadas in the one-star or no-star categories. A bed in a room without bath, shared with two or three others, can be had for as little as $2 or $3.

One notch above these budget accommodations are the two-star hotels, which are still fairly Spartan. Though often located in old colonial houses, they generally have a private bath in every room. They attract a slightly older and less budget-conscious clientele, willing to spend around $10 or $12 for a double room with bath. At the top of the local scale are the three-star hotels catering mostly to the tour groups, to the foreign middle-aged and older persons traveling by car, and to the Mexican vacationers. In basic comfort, they offer little more than the two-star hotels, but they cost between two and three times as much. They are somewhat better kept up, and rooms are equipped with telephone and television. Both two- and three-star hotels usually have a restaurant as well. Once chosen, the hotel becomes the tourist's home base, main point of reference in town, and the main source of local information, either from the hotel staff or from fellow guests met on the patio, in the lobby, or in the restaurant.

Restaurants are chosen much like hotels, by personal inspection and by recommendation of either guidebooks or other tourists, with perhaps greater emphasis on the latter. Consequently, half a dozen restaurants have come to cater predominantly or even almost exclusively to foreign tourists and resident gringos, and have become meeting places for different crowds of expatriates—for example, La Familia for unconventional, countercultural youths, Madre Tierra for the Canadians, Britons, and Americans, El Fogón de Jovel for the guided tours, El Teatro for the gourmet, El Tuluk for the "best buyers," and so on. Some restaurants and cafés are connected with art and craft galleries, art cinemas, bookstores, and other "high culture" activities; some offer live music in the evening, and display a multilingual bulletin board advertising art films, boutiques, puppies, apartments for rent, rides to the United States, and so on. In short, they become almost social clubs where tourists can meet resident gringos and local Mexican writers, artists, and intellectuals. In the last few years, San Cristóbal has developed an embryonic café society, with a floating crowd of passing tourists on its fringe. The sophisticated ethnic tourist gets much information from these social centers if he stays a few days.

Finally, shops are also points of encounter between tourists and middlemen. The buying behavior in shops is quite different from what it is in the Indian craft market. At the top of the scale, La Segoviana, the cooperatives, and more exclusive boutiques tag their wares and openly discourage haggling with a multilingual sign advertising fixed prices. Many more modest stores accept bargaining and do not use price tags. Tourists are no more competent in bargaining with ladino shopkeepers than with Indians, but they are more unrestrained by feelings of guilt in doing so and feel freer to engage openly in comparison shopping. Ladino-owned stores, since they have more overhead, have somewhat higher minimum selling prices than the Chamula outdoor vendors, but offer a much wider range and better quality of wares. For authentic Indian weavings, however, their best prices are often 20 or 30 percent lower than in the Indian-run cooperatives with fixed prices.

So far, we have spoken of middlemen as if they were all ladinos. Almost all are, but a smaller number of expatriates (often married to Mexicans) also run a few hotels and shops, and thus regularly come in contact with tourists. They capitalize on their fluent English or French to attract a more upscale clientele and they gravitate toward the galleries, which become expatriate hangouts and informal tourist information centers and social clubs. In fact, these foreign entrepreneurs are connecting links between transient foreign tourists and the rest of the resident gringo community, who constitute a little social world of their own.

Tourists, tourees, and middlemen are three abstract categories of interacting actors in the tourist trade. The analysis so far has left out four important facts, however.

First, the bulk of the ladino town population do not belong to any of these groups. They are clearly not tourists, nor are they exotic enough culturally to become tourees; finally, if they are not involved in the tourist trade, they are not middlemen either. They are simply regular townspeople, going about their normal lives as teachers, pupils, housewives, craftsmen, civil servants, tradesmen, and so on, and interacting mostly with each other rather than with tourists. Yet tourism has become so pervasive in San Cristóbal that it has left hardly anyone unaffected.

Tourists, for example, have no monopoly on observation. They are also being observed. Tourist watching by locals on the Zócalo has become an added evening attraction. Local tastes, attitudes, and visions of the world are affected by these contacts. At the limit, the tourist becomes a touree to the locals! At a minimum, he is a vector of outside influences, styles, tastes, values, and so on.

Tourism powerfully sucks San Cristóbal into the global village. San Cristóbal is no longer a small provincial town on the extreme periphery of a poor, dependent Latin American country. It is a pole of attraction to hundreds of thousands of foreign visitors who, in turn, tell hundreds of thousands more about it. Its boutiques carry the latest styles of clothes, or almost. Its art cinemas show arcane Czech or French films in the original (to admittedly small audiences). Its youth dances to the latest North American tunes. It will, in short, never be the same again.

The second point is so trivially obvious that it barely needs to be stated: much, if not most, interaction takes place *within* each group rather than *between* them. This is true even of the tourists in spite of their transience, and of the fact that they come from many different ethnic groups. We have perhaps not dwelt enough on the strange, ambivalent relationship that links tourists with one another. Tourists both repel and attract one another. Their presence not only spoils the prices and the natives, but it is living evidence to other tourists that their very search for authenticity is in jeopardy. The more tourists a place has, the less "real" it becomes. "Authentic" and "touristy" are antithetical adjectives.

Yet tourists, even the hardier, more independent strain, have obvious advantages in seeking each other's company. Vital, up-to-date information can be reliably shared, and costly, dangerous mistakes avoided. Lodging or transport costs can be lowered by banding together. A chance encounter can turn into a romance or a lasting friendship. Conversation with fellow travelers and exchanges of experiences can fill boring hours on a slow bus. The possibilities are boundless. One may yearn for *dépaysement*, but, in the last analysis, one feels most at home with oneself and with one's "own kind."

Third and most important, ladino-Indian relations have been transformed, in part because of tourism. Many changes would have taken place with or without tourism, simply as by-products of "modernization." For instance, the increase in both literacy and bilingualism in Spanish among Indians accompanied the spread of rural schools and the migratory labor system which forced Indian men to work far from home on plantations, construction sites, oil fields, and so on. Even some changes that might be thought to have been responses to tourist tastes are in fact endogenous in origin. One example is evolution of Zinacanteco dress style from very sober white cloth with just a pin-stripe of pink to a much more colorful explosion of pink with multicolored embroidered flowers. To be sure, tourists do find the new style attractive, but relatively few Zinacantecas commercialize their weavings, and only a handful of women sell them in town. It was Zinacanteco tastes which drove the changes, which accompanied a transformation of the rural economy from growing maize to the commercial production of flowers in plastic hothouses (Collier and Mountjoy 1988). When Zinacantecos began growing flowers, they started embroidering flowers on their clothes.

What has changed as a consequence of tourism, however, is the attitude of ladinos toward Indians. Before the advent of mass tourism, ladino-Indian relations could best have been characterized as colonial and paternalistic (Colby and van den Berghe 1961; Colby 1966; van den Berghe and Colby 1961). Ladinos looked down on Indians as an obstacle to the development of Mexico, as an embarrassing reminder that Mexico was not yet a fully modern nation, and as a large, inert mass of backward, primitive peasants who stubbornly refused to become "civilized"—that is, to speak Spanish and behave like *gente de razón* ("reasonable or rational people," as the ladinos called themselves in contradistinction to Indians).

Ladinos, by contrast, considered themselves to be the heirs to Spanish civilization—the only one whose values they accepted unquestioningly. Speaking Spanish and being civilized were coterminous. Unlike other parts of Mexico where, at least among the intelligentsia, there is an ideology of *mestizage*, a cult of the Indian past and a depreciation of the Spanish colonial period, in San Cristóbal the elite have always been conservative, Eurocentric, proudly Spanish and colonial, and almost defiantly regionalist and un-Mexican. San Cristóbal is said to be unique among Mexican towns in having a monument to its conquistador (fig. 5). The Indian population surrounding the town was simply looked at as "our Indians,"—the rustic peasants who, as a matter of course, had been feeding the urban ladinos for the last four hundred years, sweeping the streets of the city clean, and otherwise performing all kinds of useful but unpleasant tasks. Indians were people who conveniently spared ladinos the indignity of tilling the soil, and who lived with them under a system of quasi-feudal patron-client ties. By contrast, the ladino upper class saw itself as a leisure class, looking down on any physical exertion, even walking in the street or carrying small parcels. A middle- or upper-class housewife buying in the market, for instance, would invariably be accompanied by a maid to carry her purchases, and upper-class men would drive even short distances rather than be seen walking in the street. A *caballero* simply had to go on horseback, or its modern equivalent.

With the advent of tourism, ladinos became increasingly aware that high status people (to whom they looked up as representatives of advanced Western countries they admired) were paying good money and spending valuable time to look, not so much at their precious colonial heritage, as at the despised, downtrodden Indians. If "civilized" people came all the way from Europe and North America to look at Indians, attend their festivals, visit their churches, trek to their villages, and learn about their weaving, it must be because Indians are interesting. San

Cristóbal, the colonial city, was slowly discovering a second vocation as a mecca of ethnic tourism.

Naturally, there was a good deal of self-interest in this ladino redefinition of their town. Indians were now a marketable commodity which ladinos were best placed to exploit. The new exploitation, however, was no longer of the Indian as a beast of burden, but as a carrier of a respected culture and producer of valuable arts and crafts. Coffee-table art books were now being published about Indian weavings (Morris 1987); old women in remote villages were attracting respectful young apprentices from North America; camera crews from European television came to film festivals; theater groups and cooperatives were being formed; collectors eagerly sought Indian weavings, which now found their way into elegant boutiques and became incorporated in fabulously expensive designer clothes. The ladino image of the brutish, inebriated Indian peasant had to be revised, and indeed it was. So, inevitably, was ladino behavior toward them. During my 1990 fieldwork, I observed only one episode of a ladino insulting Indians (a boy of about ten called two adult Chamula men *burros*). A couple of decades ago, this kind of behavior was common.

This change of attitude is evident all over San Cristóbal. The majority of better-class hotels and restaurants now use Indian motifs and artifacts in creating a local ambiance attractive to tourists. Five of the hotels have large mural paintings depicting archaeological themes from Palenque or Bonampak, contemporary Indians in local dress superimposed on a Chiapas map, or a village scene from San Juan Chamula (figs. 40, 41). Nearly all the hotels above the one-star category use Indian handicrafts to decorate their lobby, hallway, restaurant, and rooms. Pottery from Amatenango features prominently as planters for tropical vegetation in the patios, while Lacandón bows and arrows and highland textiles and straw hats decorate walls. Even in the cheaper posadas and one-star hotels where investment in decoration is kept to a minimum, one finds Chiapas tourism posters featuring Indians.

The walls of the tourism office itself are virtually covered with posters and photographs of Indians, and with Indian textiles and other artifacts (figs. 30, 31), as is true of the travel agencies and most of the score or so of better restaurants catering mostly to tourists. (Among the better restaurants, a few, such as El Teatro, La Parilla, El Unicornio, and the two Chinese restaurants, have different themes, however.) El Fogón de Jovel carries the Indian theme to the extent of dressing up its ladino personnel as Indians.

Counting the kinds of postcards on the stands of tourist shops is also a revealing indicator, since postcards (many of them, in artistic black and white, by local photographers) are quickly responsive to tourist demand. On the five stands I inventoried, Indians were featured 147 times; landscapes, 78 times; archaeology, 26 times; colonial architecture, 23 times; and fauna or flora, 7 times. Indians were, again, the hands-down favorites.

Museums likewise reflect a growing ladino consciousness of Indians as a central and valued component of the region's history and culture. the two largest private collections open to the public (Na Bolom and Sergio Castro's) are devoted almost entirely to the Indian present and past. The INAH museum has an archaeology room on the main floor, and the upper story is devoted almost entirely to Indian textiles. Even the main downstairs hall, the theme of which is colonial San Cristóbal, makes ample room for the role of Indians in colonial history, and treats the Indian contribution to it both respectfully and sympathetically.

Perhaps most revealing of changing ladino attitudes is the increasing use of Indian names and of signs in Tzotzil. The term "Jovel" (from the Tzotzil word *Jobel,* meaning "grass," itself a translation of San Cristóbal's original Nahuatl name, *Zacatlán,* "place of grass"), was never used by ladinos until a decade or so ago. Now it features in the name of a restaurant and of a posada, and is even used in common ladino parlance. Restaurants, hotels, textile cooperatives, travel agencies, and other commercial establishments use Indian names like Pakal, Tuluc, Moxviquil, Xaman, Bonampak, Kubul Can, and others. The "open" sign on the restaurant door of the hotel where I stayed is quadrilingual, with Tzotzil as the fourth language. Admittedly, most of this name-giving has ulterior commercial motives, but it also unequivocally shows that, at the very least, local ladinos recognize Indian culture as a valuable asset, and as an enrichment—not, as before, an embarrassment— of their sense of Mexican nationhood.

A fourth and final effect of tourism on social relations deserves at least a brief mention, even though my study was not focused on it. It concerns a profound change in gender relations, at least among the

Chamula. The commercialization of handicrafts for tourists has been almost entirely controlled by women who are both the producers and the sellers, and who therefore control a new source of income. Especially in recent years, when the oil bust and economic depression left many Indian men unemployed, this new income was vital to many poor families. Rus (1990), for instance, reports that in a Chamula community of 246 households she studied in detail, K'at'ixtik, no household was selling textiles to tourists in 1976, while in her 1987–88 economic census 42 percent did.

To be sure, Chamulas have entered that textile market to a greater extent than other groups, and K'at'ixtik may not be representative. But at a minimum, several thousand women and their families in the region derive *some* income from tourism. For the two or three hundred women who regularly sell their own work and that of others to tourists in San Juan Chamula or San Cristóbal itself, the income is substantial, despite relatively low profit margins. While no one, to my knowledge, has yet become rich, for many families the tourist trade has made the difference between subsistence and starvation. This tourist trade has also given much more leverage to women vis-à-vis their husbands, many of whom are now driven off from even low-paying day-labor jobs in *fincas* and construction sites by Guatemalan immigrants who will work even more cheaply. A common disgruntled comment by both Indian men and women (especially among the Chamula, who have always been poorer than other groups because of land scarcity and an exploding population) is that nowadays men are just useless hangers-on, who cannot provide for their families anymore.

Tourism, in short, has profoundly affected social relations in San Cristóbal and beyond. It had rendered even more complex a preexisting system of ethnic relations between the dominant ladinos and the subordinate Indians. By and large, these relations have become less feudal and more open. Ladinos, as middlemen in the tourist trade, have benefited from it far more than Indians have, but there has been some trickle-down effect for Indians as well. Furthermore, ladino attitudes toward Indians have improved as a consequence of tourism. At a minimum, one can say that no one is *worse* off because of tourism. Unlike the situation in many coastal resorts, for instance, no one has been displaced by tourism. San Cristóbal is still firmly in local hands, and the tourists are not about to take it over. On balance, then, tourism has been a good thing for San Cristóbal, an assessment in which nearly all my informants concurred. In the final chapter, I shall try to explain why San Cristóbal was such a success story in tourism development, and to draw some policy implications from that success.

WHAT WENT RIGHT?

8 TOURISM AND SOCIAL CHANGE

Ethnic tourism is, by nature, a fragile commodity. Its successful long-term exploitation requires a delicate and highly vulnerable balance of factors which can be easily disrupted by greed. Simply stated, the problem is that ethnic tourism is intrinsically self-destroying unless carefully controlled. Places and people attract ethnic tourists to the extent that they are exotic, authentic, and "unspoiled." As we have seen in Chapter 5, the charm of a place spreads in large part through word-of-mouth, either between tourists during their current trip or between friends or family members planning trips back home. Word-of-mouth, however, works both ways. When the word gets around that Shangri-la is no longer what it used to be, there are plenty of alternatives.

The irony, evident to most ethnic tourists themselves, is that they are often the principal source of the "spoilage," along with other forces of "modernization" and "development." Hence the dilemma: consciously develop ethnic tourism by building a large infrastructure of luxurious accommodations and the resultant quick and easy access may kill the goose that lays the golden eggs. The successful maintenance or expansion of ethnic tourism thus requires a sensitive type of development strategy, and one antithetical to the main thrust of the Mexican government's emphasis on "intensive modernization of hotel facilities to provide deluxe services; and the increase in technology which confers advantages to huge economic conglomerates over small, family-owned hotels" (Hiernaux and Rodriguez 1990: 7–8). Up to a certain point, the tourist traffic can be safely increased by providing better access and comfortable, clean hotels, restaurants, and other amenities. But certain conditions must be preserved:

1. Tourist traffic must not exceed a crucial saturation point. While it is impossible to determine exactly what that point is, I would suggest a one percent rule: ethnic tourists, at any given time, must not exceed one percent of the locals. Naturally, this is no exact prescription, for among other things, the size of the community is an important factor: the smaller a town, the more vulnerable it is to uncontrollable and irreversible damage. An Indian village of 3,000 receiving a daily flow of 30 tourists will probably be more drastically affected than a city of 3,000,000 with an influx of 30,000. In the large city, much of the modernity *precedes* the tourist influx, whereas in the small village it *accompanies* it. Moreover, some small and medium-size cities inevitably receive a disproportionate flow of tourists compared to the large cities, especially in Mexico, where tourists flock to a dozen coastal resorts, an equal number of inland colonial towns, and a handful of the largest and most accessible archaeological sites. Within that limited number of locations, tourists further increase their visibility by concentrating in the center of town and around a small number of "attractions," such as museums, ruins, churches, and the like. Even a one percent presence can loom oppressively large. San Cristóbal is now very close to that perilous threshold.

2. The development of facilities must be kept as invisible as possible. The place must be made to seem as pristine and unchanged as possible.

Development must take as far as possible the form of restoration rather than construction. Commercialization must be discrete. Stringent restrictions on the size and style of building and publicity signs must be rigorously enforced. In short, a successful center of ethnic tourism must achieve the difficult—indeed, seemingly impossible—feat of developing while keeping its pristine look. It must develop, but seem not to do so.

3. To make matters more difficult yet, the successful ethnic tourist center must avoid "museumization," "Disneylandization," and "boutiquization"; that is, it must keep its authenticity. It is not enough that it look pretty; it must remain *real*. Its inhabitants must not seem to be extras in a period film, but real people leading normal lives. Its houses must look lived in, its churches prayed in, its markets traded in, and by locals. The trouble with the conception of "living museums" is that they quickly become dead. The town must avoid becoming a decor. Its shops must resist becoming trendy galleries and "artsy-craftsy" boutiques, more reminiscent of a Santa Fe, New Mexico, or San Antonio, Texas, mall than of a Third World town.

"Staged authenticity," as MacCannell (1973, 1976) calls it, is, of course, a difficult act to perform, especially with ethnic tourists who are a discriminating clientele, both wary and weary of manipulation. Yet laissez-faire is no recipe for success, because the combined impact of modernity and individual greed can quickly ruin the charm of a small town. The successful ethnic tourism center must be planned and controlled, but sensitively and on a small scale, by knowledgeable people. Central state planning is obviously not a success formula either. The only model compatible with this special kind of tourism is one based on local control at the municipal level, combined with small-scale private enterprise and investment. Both the political and the economic control must remain in the hands of long-term residents with both knowledge of and concern for their town. Local control and enterprise also ensure that money spent locally remains in town and trickles down.

As of the period of this study, San Cristóbal has been remarkably successful in becoming a major pole of tourist attraction without becoming at the same time *too* touristy. To be sure, a few of the more discriminating purists among the ethnic tourists have already complained that San Cristóbal is not as "good" as they remember it from earlier visits, or more touristy than comparable Guatemalan towns, such as Quetzaltenango or Huehuetenango. Yet even those who apply the most stringent criteria of authenticity in their evaluation of the quality of their tourist experience still overwhelmingly find San Cristóbal "better" than most towns in Mexico, or even "the best town" in Mexico.

A few of the more perceptive tourists cannot help but notice that the food in the better restaurants is adapted to their taste, that the menus are often multilingual, that some of the hotels are built in *neo*colonial style, that proliferating galleries of cute boutiques sell nonlocal crafts, that, in short, authenticity is already being staged. However, the overwhelming impression remains one of a "real" town where most people lead "normal" lives, almost as if the tourists were not there. For the most part, San Cristóbal has preserved its "typical" character. It reproduces, in stone and in flesh, the mental image that the tourist has of what a traditional, unspoiled Mexican town *should* look like. By and large, it did so by remaining itself, rather than by remaking itself into a Disneyland. To be sure, San Cristóbal spruced itself up. If anything, it looks prettier, cleaner, more sanitized than it was twenty or thirty years ago (figs. 26, 27, 28, 29). Several churches have been carefully restored; old colonial patios that had fallen into disrepair are now freshly whitewashed; a few more stone fountains have been added here and there; decorative plants, local pottery, caged parrots, and Maya-inspired murals now adorn hotels and restaurants (figs. 40, 41); and many shops, most hotels, and some restaurants cater almost exclusively to tourists. Still, nine-tenths of the town, and, most obviously, the sprawling produce market, are quite visibly and convincingly real, in the sense that they would be there, unchanged, with or without tourists.

In spite of creeping "boutiquization" (for example, a bakery featuring baguettes calls itself La Boutique del Pan), San Cristóbal is now probably at the peak of its attractiveness to ethnic tourists. It is still authentic, but it also offers enough distractions to keep a young tourist amused for several days, after exhausting the list of museums, markets, churches, and nearby Indian villages. There is live music in one or more restaurants every evening; a regular cinema showing feature films (many in English with Spanish subtitles); an art cinema showing ethnographic or esoteric foreign films; frequent slide shows, talks, theatrical performances, or concerts at the INAH museum, Na Bolom, or the Casa de Las Imágenes; and at least three or four decent bookstores with good browsing if one reads Spanish. All these sources of entertainment are either free or available for an admission fee of one dollar or less. And, of course, the possibilities for stimulating conversation or flirtation in a cosy café over a delicious thirty-five-cent espresso or a strong fifty-cent beer are endless. Perhaps the only other Mexican town of comparable size that could compete with San Cristóbal in terms of both well-restored authenticity and creature comforts is Pátzcuaro in the state of Michoacán, but its surrounding peasant population is much more westernized and mestizoized.

The reasons for San Cristóbal's success are thus not far to seek:

1. The town is sufficiently accessible by paved road and by scheduled bus service, yet the absence of a jet airport has screened out the great hordes of extremely hurried tourists. This seems to be the optimal degree of access for a successful center of ethnic tourism.

2. San Cristóbal is sufficiently far away from comparably attractive towns to leave the road traveler with few options for an overnight stay. It is simply difficult to see much of San Cristóbal on the way to any other overnight destination, nor does it make much sense to try: Tuxtla is a hot, modern city lacking nearby attractions, except for the Cañón del Sumidero; Comitán is much smaller, less attractive, and more provincial than San Cristóbal; Palenque is 200 kilometers away; so are the nearest Guatemalan tourist destinations; other small towns nearby, such as Ocosingo, lack the minimum infrastructure of hotels to attract all but the hardiest.

3. San Cristóbal is intrinsically attractive for four principal reasons: its Indianness, its colonial ambiance, its temperate climate, and its mountain scenery. It lacks only a major nearby archaeological site; but it is on the way to Palenque, and the nearer site of Toniná could easily be made more accessible by paving some fifteen kilometers. Even though tourists come primarily to see Indians, San Cristóbal also attracts people with other interests, and offers ethnic tourists several additional bonuses which help spread its reputation as one of the best towns (if not *the* best) in Mexico.

4. Because San Cristóbal is primarily a center of *ethnic* tourism, it has attracted a relatively nonpolluting type of tourist, in both the physical

and the cultural sense. In the physical sense, ethnic tourists do not demand the kind of facilities, characteristic of coastal resorts, which put a heavy strain on the environment. Culturally, ethnic tourists tend to be more adaptable, sensitive, and tolerant; they do not seek to import their culture and "take over" a town, thus alienating their hosts.

5. Tourism development in San Cristóbal has been successful because it was under local political control, largely free of central government planning, and based principally on small-scale, local, private investment. Much of the development was the initiative of the local bourgeoisie, who had the acumen and taste to restore buildings they already owned (often through inheritance) and to convert them to commercial use as hotels or restaurants, but who also lacked the capital to attempt anything more grandiose. (Only the Bonampak Hotel along the Pan-American Highway falls into the more ambitious, and less successful, category: it has a Tex-Mex appearance, more in tune with the suburbs of Houston than with San Cristóbal.)

In short, a good deal of the success of San Cristóbal is attributable to the fact that the development was not centrally planned, but that it was locally controlled by restrictive building codes. Development took off in the late 1970s, but despite its relatively fast pace, San Cristóbal grew almost organically, out of the existing old town center, under the initiative of a multiplicity of small, local entrepreneurs with limited capital, but with a good knowledge of the local situation, a good understanding of what attracted tourists, and sufficient adaptability to cater to a wide range of tastes. Local entrepreneurs collectively possessed a store of knowledge and skills for which no amount of large-scale central planning can be a substitute. The larger the scale of development, the more irreversible and potentially catastrophic the mistakes can be. Small scale means, at worst, small correctible mistakes.

Small-scale enterprise brings several other advantages, especially in a low wage, high unemployment economy. It is labor intensive, and provides many jobs to local people, and relatively more skilled jobs than the large chain hotels, for example. (Twenty small hotels require twenty times as many managers as one large one.) Small enterprises pay relatively low wages but provide more secure employment, as recruitment to jobs relies more heavily on friendship and kinship networks.

Nephews, brothers, and cousins cannot be fired as easily when business is down. Finally, small businesses have lower overhead, and thus are better able to weather the ups and downs of a highly seasonal and volatile trade like tourism. An owner-operated ten-room hotel with a staff of six, including the owner's wife and two children, who live in a couple of back rooms, can stand two or three months of 25 percent occupancy better than a debt-riddled 250-room behemoth with a staff of 150. Small is not only beautiful, it is also often more cost efficient and more recession proof.[1]

Some evidence for my small-makes-sense thesis is provided by the Hiernaux and Rodríguez study (1990:14–15), at least in the area of job creation. They contrast, for example, Quintana Roo and Guerrero, states which received a massive infusion of federal pesos in luxury coastal resorts, with Veracruz, which received little. Quintana Roo accounted in 1988 for 3.2 percent of Mexican direct tourism employment and Guerrero for 6.4 percent, but Veracruz, with little state investment, fell in between with 4.3 percent. All the beach resorts together accounted for only 17 percent of tourist jobs in Mexico despite having received the lion's share of government support. They also argue that seasonal unemployment is more pronounced in the luxury coastal resorts than in the rest of the hospitality industry.

The reasons for San Cristóbal's success also contain clear warnings, especially for the kind of unthinking boosterism that seems to prevail not only among the San Cristóbal entrepreneurial elite but also at all levels of government. It is, of course, difficult to be riding a boom without believing that it will never stop, and that more can only mean better. Up to a point, business success rides on optimism, to be sure, and San Cristóbal suffers no shortage of optimists. Several of the hotels are busy building expansions in their back lots. A large new multistore

1. For another study documenting the beneficial total impact of small-scale, indigenous entrepreneurship on tourism development, see Kottak (1983). Despite Kottak's title (*Assault on Paradise*), he admits that the pretourist "paradise" was more in the tourist's imagination than in the grim economic reality, and he documents a general rise in economic standards and dramatic upward mobility of some local families in his Brazilian fisherman's community.

gallery is being built next to an existing one on Guadalupe Street. Rumors circulate about the Club Méditerranée's intent to build a large hotel on a site it already owns on the periphery of town; the prospect is usually greeted favorably on the presumption that it will attract more and richer tourists, and not compete with existing hotels. The rising tide of the tourist bonanza, it is widely assumed, will lift all shops, restaurants, and hotels.

Two most common complaints recur among those who live from tourism. The first concerns the lack of a nearby jet airport. The nearest one, in Tuxtla, eighty kilometers away, is located (because of political corruption, it is rumored) on a site which is frequently foggy. Canceled flights produce disgruntled passengers and wary tour operators, and potential clientele is turned away from San Cristóbal, it is alleged. Local boosters try to pressure the federal government to build a jet airport nearby, but the valley of Jovel is almost entirely built up, and the rugged terrain around it precludes a nearby site. Perhaps the main bone of contention is access to the Maya ruin of Palenque, which, though in the state of Chiapas, can be reached more quickly from Villahermosa in the state of Tabasco. A Chiapas resource, it is argued, to which San Cristóbal could be the gateway, is being unjustly "seized" by a neighboring state. (The obvious counter to that argument is that even with an airport in San Cristóbal, Palenque would still be 200 kilometers away. Clearly the best gateway to Palenque would be to build an airport there!)

The second recurrent complaint is linked to the first one: that San Cristóbal predominantly receives *turismo pobre*, "poor tourism." The proportion of rich tourists could be increased, it is alleged, if San Cristóbal were to have a jet airport and international class hotels. The "turismo pobre" statement is based, as I suggested in Chapter 5, on a misinterpretation of foreign tourists' spending behavior, and a misunderstanding of the nature of ethnic tourism. Ethnic tourists are not poor, they are "slumming"; that is, for the most part they could afford to spend more than they do, but are quite content to live simply (Cohen 1982a; Riley 1988; Vogt 1976).

To those who bemoan the prevalence of poor tourism, lack of luxury development, and poor access, five counterarguments can be advanced:

1. Ethnic tourists are a very special clientele attracted by *lack* of

luxury development and access by air. If one chooses to develop in that direction, one kills ethnic tourism.

2. Even if one provided luxury hotels and if ethnic tourists continued to come, they would not use the five-star facilities, because they are trying to get away from the consumer society, and want to get close to the people.

3. Centers of ethnic tourism seldom have the kinds of attraction (notably a coastline) which luxury, package-tour travelers seek. A highland town in the middle of a densely populated valley, like San Cristóbal, would not appeal to a Club Méditerranée clientele that wants to surf, swim, ride horses, or play golf—as well insulated from the natives as possible. Club Meds create the very antithesis of what ethnic tourists seek: a sanitized, hedonistic, tropical fantasyland, with the natives as shadowy servants in the background.

4. While ethnic tourists spend much less per day than the luxury tour clientele, they stay much longer in Mexico, and thus leave much more money behind than might first appear. (For evidence on the impact of low budget travelers in other parts of the world, see Cohen 1982a; Riley 1988; and Vogt 1976.) In terms of the effect on the Mexican economy, it matters little whether a tourist spends $1,500 in fifteen days or in sixty days, to use average figures suggested by the present study.

5. More of the money spent by "poor" tourists stays in Mexico and "trickles down" than is the case with the guests of international chain hotels that typically export most of their profits. Ethnic tourists stay in small hotels, eat in modest restaurants, and buy necessities in local stores. They live in a world of grubby, small-denomination banknotes rather than plastic cards. Not only does more of their money stay with locals; it also circulates *faster* and in more modest hands than the plastic kind.

Let me conclude with an argument and a plea. The argument is that, in sheer economic cost-benefit terms, ethnic tourism is really much more profitable and beneficial to a greater number of people than it seems at first blush, and that is produces little environmental or cultural pollution. Conversely, the manna of luxury coastal tourism brings much less than it seems: many profits are exported; it benefits far fewer people; and its environmental and cultural costs are staggering.

The plea is simply this: do not destroy a successful center of ethnic tourism through overdevelopment and overinvestment of the wrong kind and origin. Keep development local, small-scale, and as invisible as possible. Remain true to your own character. Do not become a bad imitation of what ethnic tourists try to escape from. Do not turn yourself into a Cancún-in-the-Mountains. First, it will not work. Second, it would be a terrible pity.

BIBLIOGRAPHY

Acerenza, Miguel Angel
  1985 *Administración del turismo.* México, D.F.: Editorial Trillas.
Adams, Kathleen M.
  1984 "Come to Tana Toraja, 'Land of the Heavenly Kings,' " *Annals of Tourism Research* 11(3):469–85.
Aguirre Beltrán, Gonzalo
  1967 *Regiones de refugio.* México: Instituto Indígenista Interamericano.
  1979 *Regions of Refuge.* Washington, D.C.: Society for Applied Anthropology. Monograph 12.
Altman, Jon
  1989 "Tourism Dilemmas for Aboriginal Australians," *Annals of Tourism Research* 16(4):456–76.
Aramberri, Julio
  1983 "El paraiso . . . perdido? Sobre algunas teorías del turismo," *Estudios Turísticos* 80:77–93.
Benjamin, Thomas
  1989 *Politics and Society in Modern Chiapas.* Albuquerque: University of New Mexico Press.
Bosselman, Fred P.
  1978 *In the Wake of the Tourist: Managing Special Places in Eight Countries.* Washington, D.C.: Conservation Foundation.
Boullon, Roberto
  1985 *Planificación del espacio turístico.* México: Trillas.
Brewer, Jeffrey D.
  1984 "Tourism and Ethnic Stereotypes: Variations in a Mexican Town," *Annals of Tourism Research* 11(3):487–501.
Britton, Robert A.
  1979 "The Image of the Third World in Tourism Marketing," *Annals of Tourism Research* 6(3):318–29.
Brosnahan, Tom, and Jane Kretchman
  1977 *Mexico and Guatemala on $10 a Day.* New York: Arthur Frommer.
Bruner, Edward M.
  1989 "Of Cannibals, Tourists and Ethnographers," *Cultural Anthropology* 4(4):438–45.
Butler, R. W., and L. A. Waldbrook
  1991 "A New Planning Tool: The Tourism Opportunity Spectrum," *Journal of Tourism Studies* 2:2–14.

Bystrzanowski, Julian, ed.

1989　*Tourism as a Factor of Change: A Sociocultural Study.* Vienna: The Vienna Centre.

Cancian, Frank

1965　*Economics and Prestige in a Mayan Community.* Stanford: Stanford University Press.

Casagrande, Louis B.

1988　"The Five Nations of Mexico," in Paul B. Goodwin, ed., *Latin America*, pp. 126–133. Guilford, Conn.: Dushkin.

Cazes, G. H.

1989　"Alternative Tourism, Reflections on an Ambiguous Concept," in *Towards Appropriate Tourism: The Case of Developing Appropriate Tourism: The Case of Developing Countries*, pp. 117–27. Frankfurt: Peter Lang Publishers.

Cohen, Erik

1972　"Toward a Sociology of International Tourism," *Social Research* 39(1):164–82.

1973　"Nomads from Affluence: Note on the Phenomenon of Drifter Tourism," *International Journal of Comparative Sociology* 14:89–103.

1974　"Who Is a Tourist? A Conceptual Classification," *Sociological Review* 22(4):527–55.

1979a　"Rethinking the Sociology of Tourism," *Annals of Tourism Research* 6(1):18–35.

1979b　"A Phenomenology of Tourist Experiences," *Sociology* 13:179–201.

1979c　"The Impact of Tourism on the Hill Tribes of Northern Thailand," *Internationales Asienforum* 10:5–38.

1982a　"Marginal Paradises, Bungalow Tourism on the Islands of Southern Thailand," *Annals of Tourism Research* 9(2):189–228.

1982b　"Thai Girls and Farang Men," *Annals of Tourism Research* 9(3):403–428.

1984　"The Sociology of Tourism: Approaches, Issues and Findings," *Annual Review of Sociology* 10:373–92.

1985　"Tourism as Play," *Religion* 15:291–304.

1987　"Alternative Tourism: A Critique," *Tourism Recreation Research* 12(2):13–18.

1988　"Authenticity and Commoditization in Tourism," *Annals of Tourism Research* 15(3):371–86.

1989　" 'Primitive and Remote,' Hill Tribe Trekking in Thailand," *Annals of Tourism Research* 16(1):30–61.

Colby, Benjamin N.

1966　*Ethnic Relations in the Chiapas Highlands of Mexico.* Santa Fe: Museum of New Mexico Press.

Colby, Benjamin N., and Pierre L. van den Berghe

1961　"Ethnic Relations in Southeastern Mexico," *American Anthropologist* 63:772–92.

1964 "Reply to Goldkind's Critique of 'Ethnic Relations in Southeastern Mexico," *American Anthropologist* 66:417–18.

1965 "Reply to Stavenhagen Critique of 'Ethnic Relations in Southeastern Mexico,'" *American Anthropologist* 67:744–46.

1969 *Ixil Country: A Plural Society in Highland Guatemala.* Berkeley: University of California Press.

Collier, George A.

1975 *Fields of the Tzotzil: The Ecological Bases of Tradition in Highland Chiapas.* Austin: University of Texas Press.

Collier, George A., and Daniel C. Mountjoy

1988 "Adaptándose a la crisis de los ochenta: Cambios socio-económicos en Apas, Zinacantán." San Cristóbal de las Casas: Instituto de Asesoria Antropológica para la Región Maya. Documento 035-II/88.

Dann, Graham, and Erik Cohen

1991 "Sociology and Tourism," *Annals of Tourism Research* 18(1):155–69.

Debbage, Keith G.

1990 "Oligopoly and the Resort Cycle in the Bahamas," *Annals of Tourism Research* 17(4):513–27.

de Kadt, Emanuel, ed.

1979 *Tourism: Passport to Development?* New York: Oxford University Press.

de la Torre Padilla, Oscar

1980 *El turismo: Fenómeno social.* México: Fondo de Cultura Económica.

de Vos, Jan

1986 *San Cristóbal: Ciudad colonial.* México: Instituto Nacional de Antropología e Historia.

Esman, Marjorie R.

1984 "Tourism as Ethnic Preservation: The Cajuns of Louisiana," *Annals of Tourism Research* 11(3):451–67.

Evans-Pritchard, Deirdre

1989 "How 'They' See 'Us': Native American Images of Tourists," *Annals of Tourism Research* 16(1):89–105.

Favre, Henri

1973 *Cambio y continuidad entre los Mayas de México.* México: Instituto Nacional Indígenista.

1985 "El Cambio Socio-Cultural y el Nuevo Indígenismo en Chiapas," *Revista Mexicana de Sociología* 47(3):161–96.

Flores Ruiz, Eduardo

1973 *Investigaciones históricas sobre Chiapas.* México, D.F.: Editorial Progreso.

Garrett, Wilbur E., and Kenneth Garrett

1989 "La Ruta Maya," *National Geographic,* October, pp. 424–79.

Getino, Octavio

1987   *Turismo y desarrollo en América Latina.* México: Editorial Limusa.

Ginier, Jean

1969   *Les touristes étrangers en France pendant l'été.* Paris: Génin.

Gobierno del Estado de Chiapas, ed.

1984   *San Cristóbal y sus alrededores.* Tuxtla Gutiérrez: Talleres Gráficos del Estado.

Goldkind, Victor

1963   "Ethnic Relations in Southeastern Mexico: A Methodological Note," *American Anthropologist* 65:394–98.

González Casanova, Pablo

1965   *La democracia en México.* México: Era.

Graburn, Nelson H. H.

1976   *Ethnic and Tourist Arts: Cultural Expressions from the Fourth World.* Berkeley: University of California Press.

1983   "The Anthropology of Tourism," *Annals of Tourism Research* 10(2):9–34.

1989   "Tourism, the Sacred Journey," in Valene L. Smith, ed., *Hosts and Guests: The Anthropology of Tourism,* pp. 17–32. Philadelphia: University of Pennsylvania Press.

Graburn, Nelson H. H., and Jafar Jafari

1991   "Tourism Social Science," *Annals of Tourism Research* 18(1):1–11.

Greenwood, D. J.

1989   "Culture by the Pound: An Anthropological Perspective on Tourism as Culture Commoditization," in Valene L. Smith, ed., *Hosts and Guests,* pp. 171–85. Philadelphia: University of Pennsylvania Press.

Harron, Sylvia, and Betty Weiler

1992   "Review: Ethnic Tourism," in Betty Weiler and Colin M. Hall, eds., pp. 83–94. *Special Interest Tourism.* London: Belhaven.

Hiernaux Nicolas, Daniel, ed.

1989   *Teoría y praxis del espacio turístico.* México: Universidad Autónoma Metropolitana.

Hiernaux Nicolas, Daniel, and Manuel Rodríguez Woog

1990   *Tourism and Absorption of the Labor Force in Mexico.* Washington, D.C.: Commission for the Study of International Migration and Cooperative Economic Development. Working Paper 34.

Huizinga, Johan

1955   *Homo Ludens: The Play Element in Culture.* Boston: Beacon Press.

Jafari, Jafar

1979   "Tourism and the Social Sciences: A Bibliography, 1970–1978," *Annals of Tourism Research* 6(2):149–94.

1984   "Unbound Ethnicity," *Tourist Review* 39:4–21.

1987   "Tourism Models: The Sociocultural Aspects," *Tourism Management,* June, pp. 151–59.

Kemper, Robert V.

1978 "Tourism in Taos and Pátzcuaro," *Annals of Tourism Research* 6(1):91–110.

1981 "Urbanization and Development in the Tarascan Region since 1940," *Urban Anthropology* 10(1):89–110.

Keyes, Charles F., and Pierre L. van den Berghe, eds.

1984 *Tourism and Ethnicity.* Special Issue of *Annals of Tourism Research* 11(3):339–501.

Kottak, Conrad P.

1983 *Assault on Paradise: Social Change in a Brazilian Village.* New York: Random House.

Laxson, Joan D.

1991 "How 'We' See 'Them': Tourism and Native Americans," *Annals of Tourism Research* 18(3):365–91.

Levy, Daniel, and Gabriel Szekely

1985 *Estabilidad y cambio: Paradojas del sistema político mexicano.* México, D.F.: El Colegio de México.

López Sánchez, Hermilo

1960 *Apuntes históricos de San Cristóbal de las Casas.* México, D.F.: Lito-Arte.

Lutkehaus, Nancy C.

1989 " 'Excuse Me, Everything Is Not All Right': On Ethnography, Film, and Representation," *Cultural Anthropology* 4(4):422–37.

MacCannell, Dean

1973 "Staged Authenticity," *American Journal of Sociology* 79(3):589–603.

1976 *The Tourist: A New Theory of the Leisure Class.* New York: Schocken. Second edition, 1989.

1984 "Reconstructed Ethnicity, Tourism and Cultural Identity in Third World Communities," *Annals of Tourism Research* 11(3):375–92.

1992 *Empty Meeting Grounds: The Tourist Papers.* London: Routledge.

Molina E., Sergio

1982 *Turismo y ecología.* México, D.F.: Editorial Trillas.

Morris, Walter F., Jr.

1984 *A Millennium of Weaving in Chiapas.* México, D.F.: Litográfica Turmex.

1987 *Living Maya.* New York: Harry N. Abrams.

Moscoso Pastrana, Prudencio

1984 *México y Chiapas: Independencia y federación de la provincia chiapaneca.* México, privately published.

Nash, Dennison

1981 "Tourism as an Anthropological Subject," *Current Anthropology* 22(5):461–68.

1984 "The Ritualization of Tourism," *Annals of Tourism Research* 11(3):503–7.

1989 "Tourism as a Form of Imperialism," in Valene L. Smith, ed., *Hosts and Guests*, pp. 37–52. Philadelphia: University of Pennsylvania Press.

Nash, Dennison, and Valene L. Smith
1991 "Anthropology and Tourism," *Annals of Tourism Research* 18(1): 12–25.

O'Rourke, Dennis
1987 *Cannibal Tours*. Los Angeles: Direct Cinema Limited.

Plog, S. C.
1974 "Why Destination Areas Rise and Fall in Popularity," *Cornell Hotel and Restaurant Administration Quarterly* 14:55–58.

Popelka, Cheryl Ann, and Mary Ann Littrell
1991 "Influence of Tourism on Handicraft Evolution," *Annals of Tourism Research* 18(3):392–413.

Porter, Daniel
1990 "Rockets of San Cristóbal: A Colonial City in the Highlands of Southern Mexico Celebrates Year Round," *New York Times*, April 15, sec. 5, pp. 14, 16.

Riley, Pamela J.
1988 "Road Culture of International Long-Term Budget Travellers," *Annals of Tourism Research* 15(3):313–28.

Romero, Hector Manuel, ed.
1988 *Enciclopedia mexicana del turismo*. México: Editorial Limosa. 20 volumes.

Rus, Diana L.
1990 *La Crisis económica y la mujer indígena: El caso de Chamula, Chiapas*. San Cristóbal de las Casas: Instituto de Asesoria Antropológica para la Región Maya, Documento de Trabajo.

Singh, Tej Vir
1989 *The Kulu Valley: Impact of Tourism Development in the Mountain Areas*. New Delhi: Himalayan Books.

Smith, Valene L., ed.
1989 *Hosts and Guests: The Anthropology of Tourism*. Philadelphia: University of Pennsylvania Press.
1992 *Pilgrimage and Tourism: The Quest in Guest*. Special Issue of *Annals of Tourism Research* 19(1):1–121.

Sontag, Susan
1977 *On Photography*. New York: Farrar, Straus and Giroux.

Stavenhagen, Rodolfo
1964 "Further Comment on Ethnic Relations in Southeastern Mexico," *American Anthropologist* 66:1155–58.

Suárez, Luís
1990 "El turismo debe ofrecer riquezas para todos," *Excelsior*, March 24.

Swain, Margaret Byrne
    1990   "Commoditizing Ethnicity in Southwest China," *Cultural Survival Quarterly* 14(1):26–29.

Turner, Louis, and John Ash
    1976   *The Golden Hordes: International Tourism and the Pleasure Periphery.* New York: St. Martin's Press.

van den Berghe, Pierre L.
    1980   "Tourism as Ethnic Relations: A Case Study of Cuzco, Peru," *Ethnic and Racial Studies* 3(6):375–91.
    1981   *The Ethnic Phenomenon.* New York: Elsevier.
    1989   *Stranger in Their Midst.* Niwot: University Press of Colorado.
    1992   "Tourism and the Ethnic Division of Labor: A Mexican Case Study," *Annals of Tourism Research* 19(2):234–49.

van den Berghe, Pierre L., and Benjamin N. Colby
    1961   "Ladino-Indian Relations in the Highlands of Chiapas, Mexico," *Social Forces* 40(1):63–71.

van den Berghe, Pierre L., and Charles F. Keyes
    1984.   "Introduction, Tourism and Re-Created Ethnicity," in *Tourism and Ethnicity.* Special Issue of *Annals of Tourism Research* 11(3):343–51.

van den Berghe, Pierre L., and George P. Primov
    1977   *Inequality in the Peruvian Andes: Class and Ethnicity in Cuzco.* Columbia and London: University of Missouri Press.

Vogt, Evon Z.
    1970   *The Zinacantecos of Mexico: A Modern Maya Way of Life.* New York: Holt, Rinehart and Winston.
    1978   *Bibliography of the Harvard Chiapas Project: The First Twenty Years, 1957–1977.* Cambridge, Mass.: Peabody Museum of Archeology and Ethnology, Harvard University.

Vogt, Evon Z., ed.
    1966   *Los Zinacantecos: Un pueblo tzotzil de los altos de Chiapas.* México, D.F.: Instituto Nacional Indígenista.

Vogt, J. W.
    1976   "Wandering, Youth and Travel Behavior," *Annals of Tourism Research* 4(2):74–105.

Volkman, Toby A.
    1982   "Tana Toraja, A Decade of Tourism," *Cultural Survival Quarterly* 6(3):30–31.
    1984   "Great Performances, Toraja Cultural Identity in the 1970s," *American Ethnologist* 11(1):152–69.

Wahab, S. E.
    1975   *Tourism Management.* London: Tourism International Press.

Wahrlich, Heide
    1984   *Tourismus: Eine Herausforderung für Ethnologen.* Berlin: Dietrich Reimer Verlag.

Wallerstein, Immanuel

1974 *The Modern World-System: Capitalist Agriculture and the Origins of the European World-Economy in the Sixteenth Century.* New York: Academic Press.

Wasserstrom, Robert

1983 *Class and Society in Central Chiapas.* Berkeley: University of California Press.

Weiler, Betty, and Colin Michael Hall, eds.

1992 *Special Interest Tourism.* London: Belhaven.

Wood, Robert E.

1984 "Ethnic Tourism, the State and Cultural Change in Southeast Africa," *Annals of Tourism Research* 11(3):353–74.

INDEX

Tabasco, 154
Tapachula, Mexico, 39, 40, 51
Taxco, 76
Tenejapa, Mexico, 65, 71, 106, 136
Teotíhuacan, Mexico, 89, 101
Textiles, 16, 51, 62–65, 69, 91, 94, 110–11, 141, 143, 145
Thailand, 99, 101, 117
Third World, 10, 15, 18, 54, 80, 81, 111, 115, 121, 137, 149
Tijuana, Mexico, 117
Toniná, Mexico, 71, 105, 151
Tourees: defined, 9; interactions with tourists, 13, 15, 18–20, 103–4, 109–12, 123–37
Tourism: addiction to, 99; domestic, 74–75, 81, 82–85, 120–21; ethnic, 7–10, 16–20, 22, 87, 91, 93, 121, 154–55; long-term, low budget, 7, 26; seasonality of, 77–78. *See also* Tourists
Tourist Office, San Cristóbal, 24, 27, 28, 32, 58, 68, 88, 143
Tourists: age and sex characteristics, 78–79; arts and crafts, 15, 27, 57, 59, 62–66, 93, 94–95, 124, 129, 139, 145; attitudes, 84–85, 96–98; attractions, San Cristóbal, 54–58, 70–71, 91–94, 96, 130; criteria of, 25–26; expenditures, 81–84, 94–96, 99, 103–17, 129; guides, 14, 23, 68–70, 115, 127, 128; guilt, 97, 104, 109, 111, 115, 121, 130, 134–35; independent, 129–37; itineraries, 77, 89–90; length of stay, 81–83, 85–86, 88, 99; nationalities, 69–70, 75–85, 95, 119–21; occupations, 80–81; sample characteristics, 78–81; saturation, 148; segregation of, 20; shops, 57, 62–65, 139; statistics, 57, 72–99; vignettes, 100–21. *See also* Tourism
Transience, 6, 19, 86, 125, 139
Transportation, 31, 35, 41, 47, 57, 73, 86–89, 136, 151

Travel agents, 14, 68–69, 113
Tula, Mexico, 89
Tulum, Mexico, 77, 89, 104, 107
Turismo pobre, 47, 49, 83, 154
Turismo social, 73
Turner, Louis, 4, 10
Tuxtla Gutiérrez, Mexico, 33, 39, 40, 51, 60, 76, 86, 87, 151, 154
Tzeltal language, 11, 29, 123
Tzotzil language, 11, 29, 59, 64, 123, 131, 144

University of Chiapas, 24, 32
University of Chicago, 42
University of Washington, 23
Uxmal, Mexico, 77, 89

van den Berghe, Pierre L., 6, 8, 9, 10, 14, 17, 21, 22, 37, 38, 123, 141
Veracruz, Mexico, 71, 89, 117, 153
Victoria, Canada, 64
Villahermosa, Mexico, 40, 71, 89, 127, 154
Vogt, Evon Z., 10, 21, 37
Vogt, J. W., 99, 154, 155
Volkman, Toby, 10

Wahab, S. E., 4
Wahrlich, Heide, 10
Waldbrook, L. A., 50
Wallerstein, Immanuel, 10
Wasserstrom, Robert, 37
Weiler, Betty, 8, 48
Wood, Robert E., 8

Yucatán, Mexico, 40, 71, 77, 86, 103, 115

Zinacantán, 21, 23, 41, 44, 62, 65, 69, 71, 93, 106, 109, 111, 114, 116, 117, 136, 141
Zócalo, San Cristóbal, 13, 25, 27, 29, 31, 41, 47, 54–58, 63, 68, 70, 93, 127, 132, 133, 140